W9-BAV-851

THE LAURA INGALLS WILDER SONGBOOK

THE LAURA INGALLS WILDER SONGBOOK

Favorite songs from the "Little House" books
compiled and edited by Eugenia Garson

Arranged for piano and guitar
by Herbert Haufrecht

Illustrated by Garth Williams

HarperCollins*Publishers*

THE LAURA INGALLS WILDER SONGBOOK

 For information address HarperCollins Children's Books, a division of HarperCollins Publishers, 10 East 53rd Street, New York, NY 10022.

Library of Congress Catalog Card Number: 68-24327
ISBN 0-06-021933-5
ISBN 0-06-021934-3 (lib. bdg.)

Table of Contents

Preface

Laura Ingalls Wilder's memories were filled with the songs of her girlhood, and so it was natural that music should have played an important part in the "Little House" books, her warmly glowing, firsthand account of family life in pioneer days. From her earliest years when Laura, her parents, her elder sister Mary, and Baby Carrie lived in a log house on the edge of the Big Woods in Wisconsin, Pa sang and played his fiddle for them. When Pa and Ma—Charles and Caroline Ingalls—packed up the covered wagon that was to carry them all farther west, the fiddle in its box was laid carefully between pillows. Its tunes lulled Laura to sleep beside the family campfires all across the plains of Kansas and into Indian country.

After a year in a log cabin on the prairie, the wagon moved them again, this time to Minnesota. Living first in a sod house dug from the banks of Plum Creek, then in the new home Pa had built nearby, Laura and Mary went to school and church for the first time. It was during this year that Mary lost her sight as the result of scarlet fever.

Another long trip, now with a new baby sister, Grace, brought them to a railroad builders' camp in Dakota Territory, where Pa became a railroader for a time. When work stopped for the winter, the Ingalls family stayed on in the surveyors' house. Here they were isolated for months until the arrival of neighbors—Mr. and Mrs. Boast—brought them company and the enjoyment of song-filled evenings.

In the spring, Pa filed his claim for a homestead near the new townsite of De Smet, South Dakota, and put up the first building in town. Then came the grim experience of the snowbound winter when Almanzo Wilder, Laura's future husband, risked his life to bring wheat to the starving settlers. Later the family settled down to summers in a claim shanty on the prairie and sheltered winters in town. While Laura taught school and helped with Mary's expenses at a college for the blind, she was being courted by Almanzo. As the eighth book of the saga concludes, Laura and Almanzo marry and go to live in a little house of their own.

There had been music of many kinds along the way: the merry tunes at Grandpa's dance back in Wisconsin, Ma's gentle hymns during lonely prairie evenings, Cousin Lena's songs at Silver Lake, and the choruses at the singing class where Almanzo was Laura's escort. Church and Sunday school, revival meetings, and patriotic celebrations had their part, as did the "Literaries"—evening gatherings that took place when the little settlement of De Smet began to grow into a community. And in hard times or good there had always been Pa's songs and the voice of the fiddle, echoing longest of all.

The Little House in the Big Woods was published in 1932; as a children's librarian I welcomed it not only as a wonderful, true story but as a reminder of the basic values so greatly needed in that time of economic depression. As I shared each succeeding volume with the boys and girls in the library, there came repeated comments and questions about the songs that were so often mentioned in the text. Favorites were greeted with delighted recognition; others were tantalizing because they were so elusive. Surely they were as real as everything else in the books! Sometimes songs were available but difficult for young people to play; sometimes words and melodies could not be found, nor was information about them easy to locate. Finally I decided to make a thorough study of all the songs that played a part in the "Little House" series.

The undertaking proved to be lengthy, interesting, and unexpectedly complex. Reference works on folk, religious, and popular music were consulted. The many subdivisions in these fields made it necessary to go through scores of volumes in order to winnow a few items of information. Some songs had never been widely known; others had attained enormous popularity in their day, only to pass into obscurity and the files of music libraries and collections; a few were known by several titles. Authors and composers were not always correctly identified; hymns were sung to many different tunes; reprinting brought changes in words and melody; and folk songs had countless versions.

Early sheet music, hymnals, song albums, and broadsides were examined and compared. Line-by-line collation was necessary where neither title nor first line was known—indeed, many older books had no indexes at all. Eventually it was possible to trace almost all the songs, with verified related data, and a generous selection appears here.

Many of Mrs. Wilder's songs were handed down through oral tradition, and her texts sometimes differed from the originals. In almost every instance her wording and punctuation have been followed. In the case of a few of the longer songs some stanzas have been dropped. Whenever information about the song, composer, or lyricist was available, I have included a brief note above the music. This is followed by a few sentences indicating where each song appears in the "Little House" series. The title of the book and the number of the page on which the song first occurs is also given. Titles are abbreviated as follows:

LHBW	*Little House in the Big Woods*
LHP	*Little House on the Prairie*
FB	*Farmer Boy*
BPC	*On the Banks of Plum Creek*
SSL	*By the Shores of Silver Lake*
LW	*The Long Winter*
LTP	*Little Town on the Prairie*
HGY	*These Happy Golden Years*

The collection offers a fascinating cross section of songs that went westward with the pioneers. There are airs deeply rooted in the Scottish and English folk tradition, as well as some with a native homespun quality. A number of these tunes were used for dancing or as singing games to be sung and stepped to without music at "play parties" in areas where, for religious reasons, dancing was frowned upon. There are patriotic songs, sentimental ballads, and rhythmic minstrel-show and music-hall melodies. Old hymns are included together with the gospel songs of the nineteenth-century revivalists. The singing school, where people sang together the music they had taken pleasure in learning, is recalled, as are the "singing families" whose concert tours were so successful during the 1840's and 1850's.

The individuality of this widely varied material, ranging from intricate choral settings to single-staff manuscript notation, has been admirably expressed in Herbert

Haufrecht's completely new arrangements, which succeed in capturing the spirit of the originals while making them invitingly easy to play and sing.

Grateful acknowledgment of their helpful cooperation is made to the librarians in the Music and Copyright divisions of the Library of Congress, particularly to Mrs. Rae Korson of the Archive of Folk Song; the Music Departments of The Free Library of Philadelphia and The Buffalo and Erie County Public Library of Buffalo, New York; the Salvation Army Library and the Union Theological Seminary Library in New York City, with special thanks to the staffs of the American History and Music Reference Divisions of the New York Public Library, where most of the work was done; and to Mr. and Mrs. L. D. Lichty, Curators of the Laura Ingalls Wilder Home and Museum in Mansfield, Missouri. Appreciation is also due the late Sigmund Spaeth, author of *A History of Popular Music in America*, James J. Fuld, author of *The Book of World-Famous Music*, and the many other authorities on American music whose published works, too numerous to mention individually, are of incalculable value to the collector.

E. G.

Home and Memories

The Beacon-Light of Home

Words by George F. St. Clair Music by H. M. Estabrooke 1879

After the Ingalls family had settled into their little claim shanty near De Smet, they rested outdoors in the beautiful spring evening. Darkness was falling softly on the prairie, and the stars came out one by one over the huge sky. Pa felt like music, and this is the song he played. SSL, *page 265*

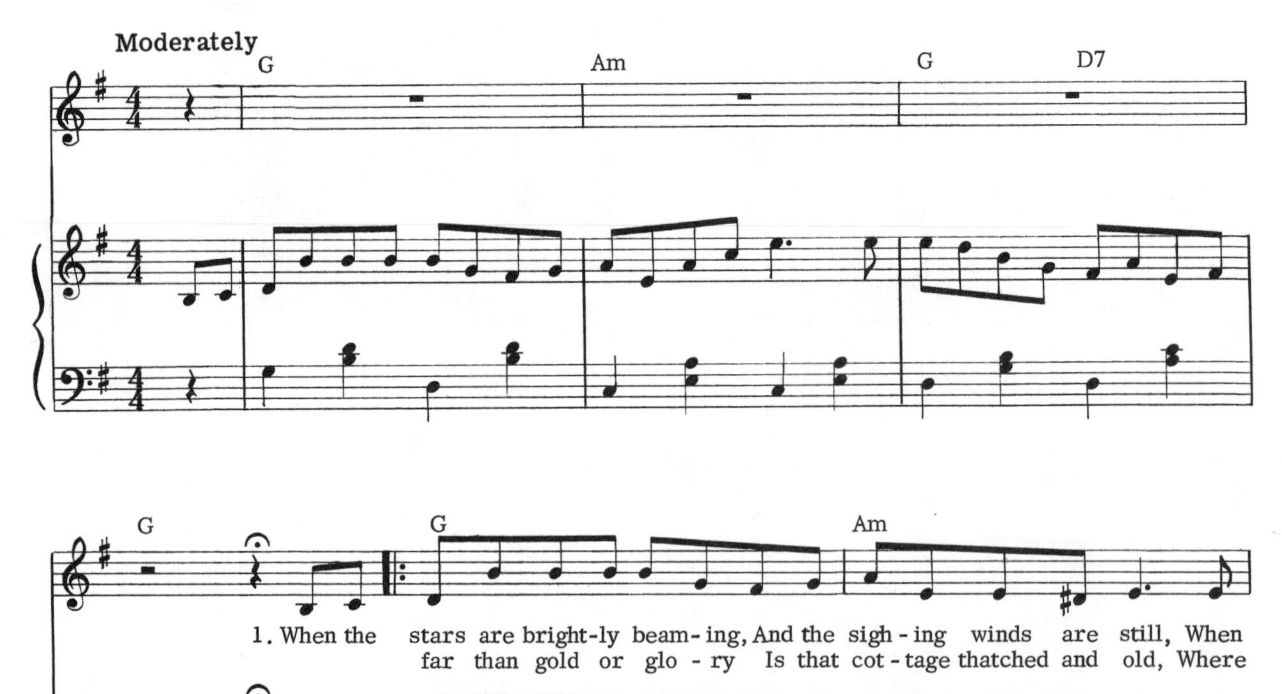

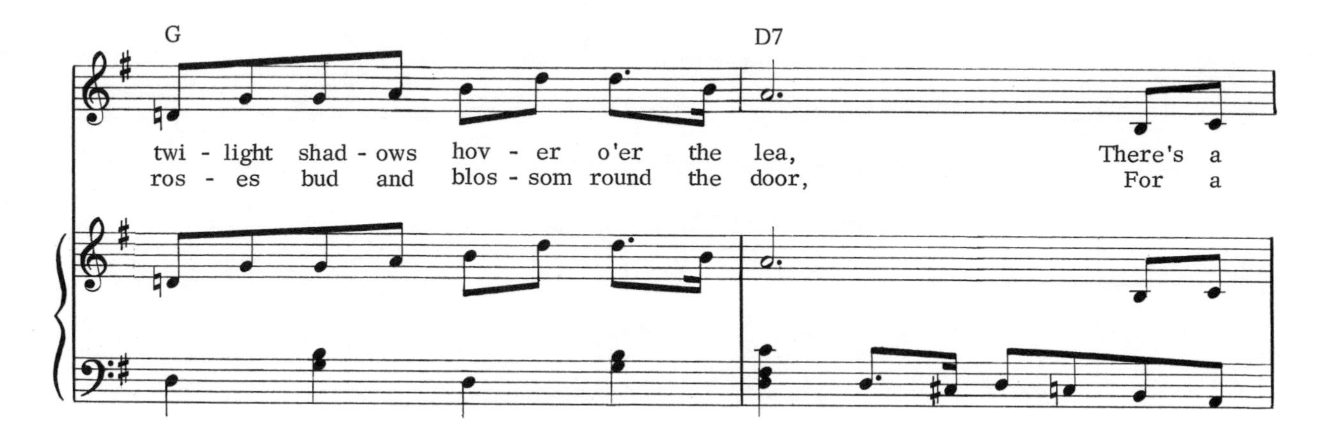
G
D7
twi - light shad - ows hov - er o'er the lea,
There's a
ros - es bud and blos - som round the door,
For a

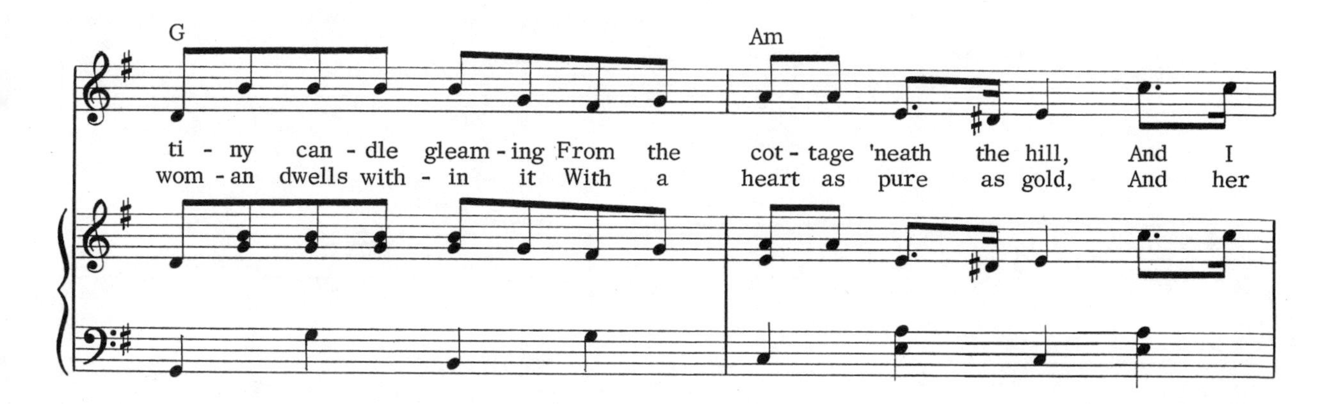
G
Am
ti - ny can - dle gleam - ing From the cot - tage 'neath the hill,
And I
wom - an dwells with - in it With a heart as pure as gold,
And her

G
D7
G
Fine
know that lit - tle bea - con shines for me.
I can
love is all my own for - ev - er - more.
When the

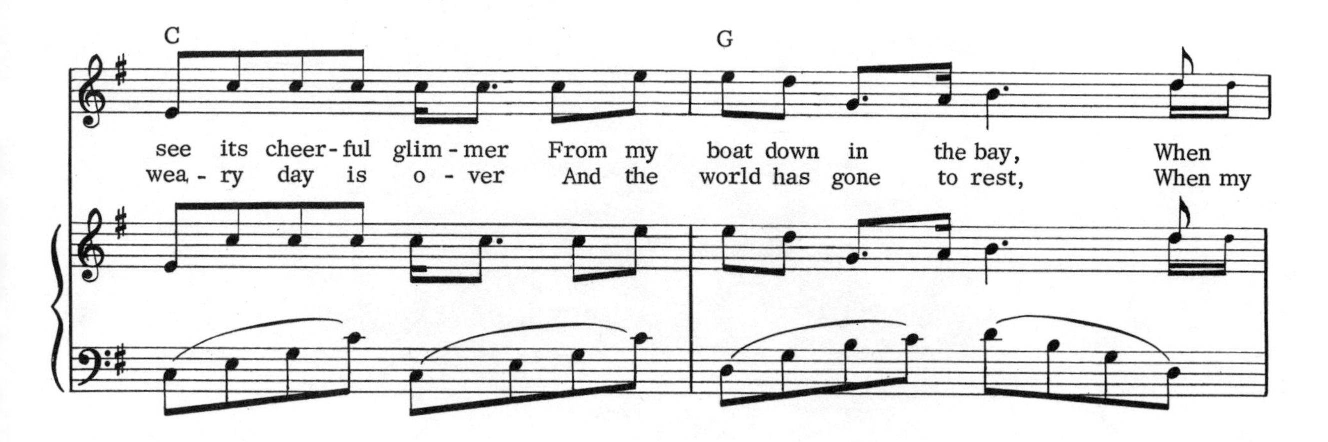
C
G
see its cheer - ful glim - mer From my boat down in the bay,
When
wea - ry day is o - ver And the world has gone to rest,
When my

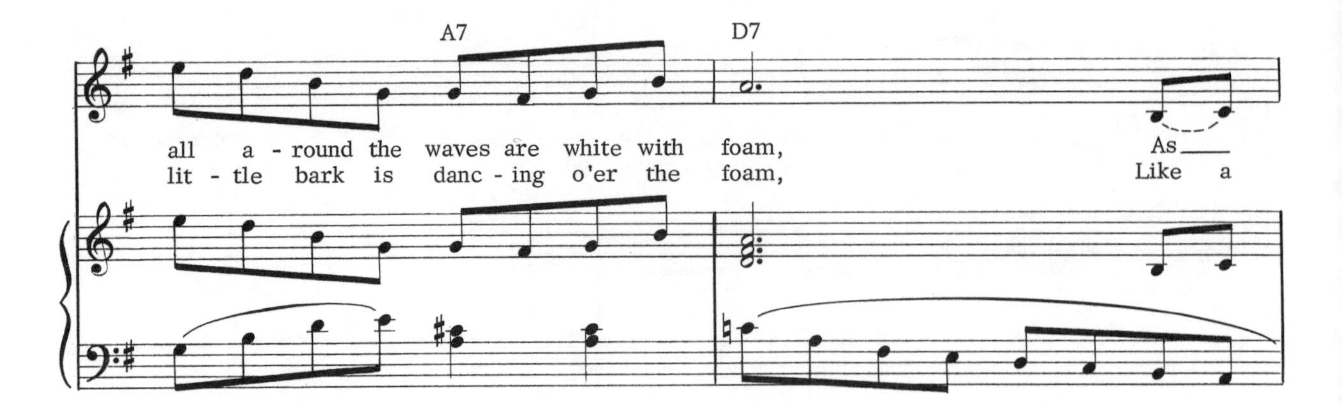
A7
D7
all a - round the waves are white with foam,
As
lit - tle bark is danc - ing o'er the foam,
Like a

G
Am
bright - ly o'er the wa - ters Comes its sun - ny lit - tle ray, A
dove at night re - turn - ing To the shel - ter of her nest, Seeks my

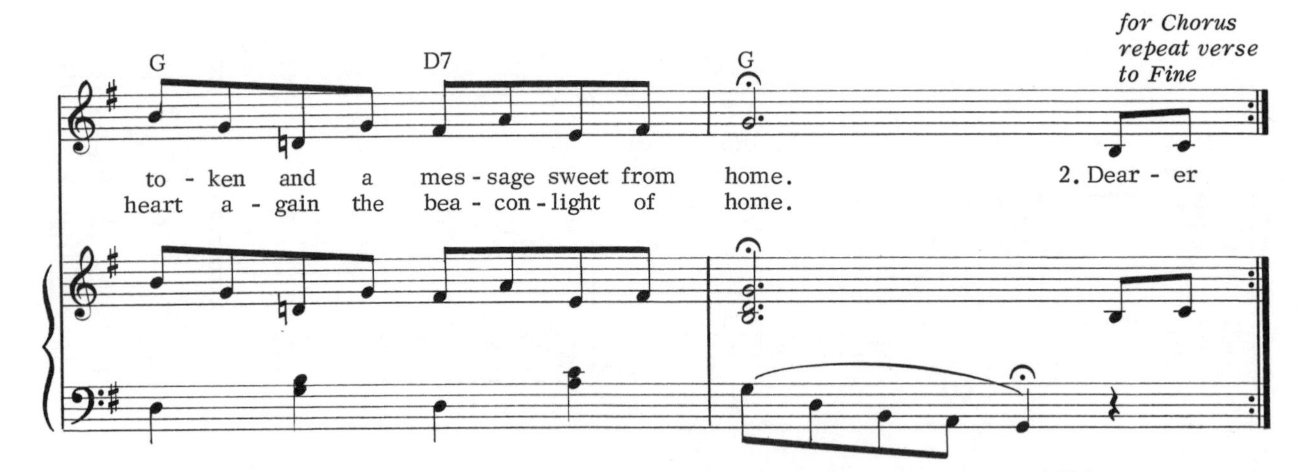
for Chorus repeat verse to Fine
G
D7
G
to - ken and a mes - sage sweet from home.
2. Dear - er
heart a - gain the bea - con - light of home.

The Floating Scow of Old Virginia

Words and Music by Charles T. White 1847

Charles T. White was a celebrated Negro singer and composer.

Pa came into the shanty with an armful of wood and said: "This wind takes your breath away. Soon as I can thaw out my fingers, we'll have a tune to drown the yowl of that wind." But when Ma heard the music, she cried: "For pity's sakes! I'd as soon listen to the wind." LW, *page 42*

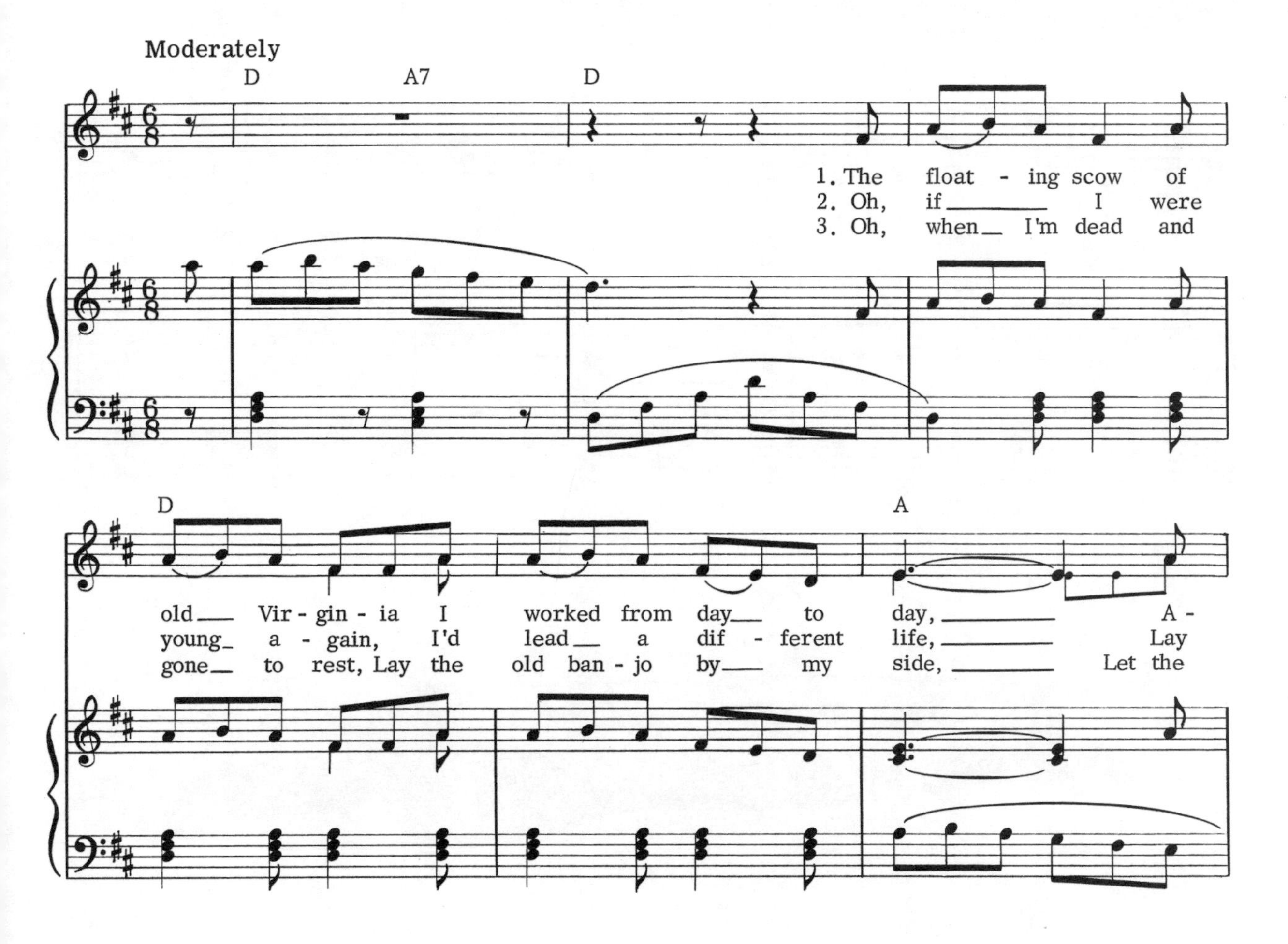

D
A7
rak - ing a - mong the oys - ter beds, To me — it was — but
up — some mon - ey and buy — some land, And take Di - nah for — my
'pos-sum and 'coon to the fu - ner - al go For they were my on - ly

D
play. But now — I'm old and fee - ble too, I
wife. But now — I'm get - ting old — and gray, I
pride. Then in soft — re - pose I'll take — my sleep, And

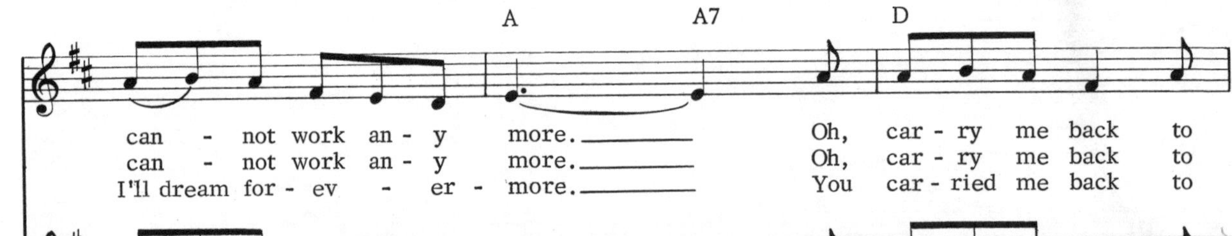
A
A7
D
can - not work an - y more. Oh, car - ry me back to
can - not work an - y more. Oh, car - ry me back to
I'll dream for - ev - er - more. You car - ried me back to

A7 D
old Vir - gin - ia, To the old Vir - gin - ia shore.
old Vir - gin - ia, To the old Vir - gin - ia shore.
old Vir - gin - ia, To the old Vir - gin - ia shore.
Chorus
G D G D
Oh, car-ry me back to old Vir-gin-ia, To old Vir-gin - ia shore, Oh,
G D A7 D
car-ry me back to old Vir-gin-ia, To old Vir-gin - ia shore.

Ben Bolt

Words by Dr. Thomas Dunn English   Music by Nelson Kneass   1848

Dr. English never received payment for this immensely popular song, and the musical accompaniment he wrote for it has been forgotten. The present melody is based on an old German tune.

When Mr. and Mrs. Boast settled in at Silver Lake, their voices rounded out the family's evenings of song. This was a favorite selection. SSL, *page 213*

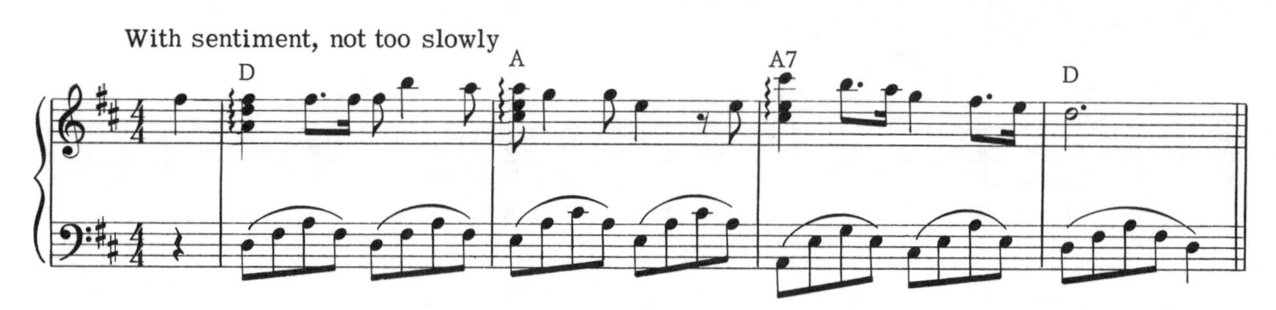

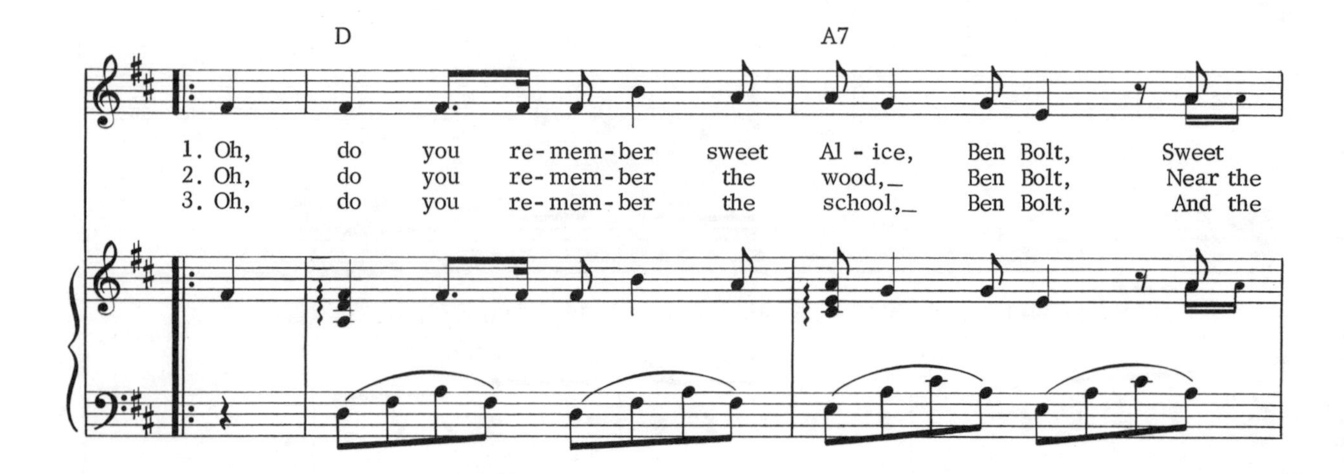

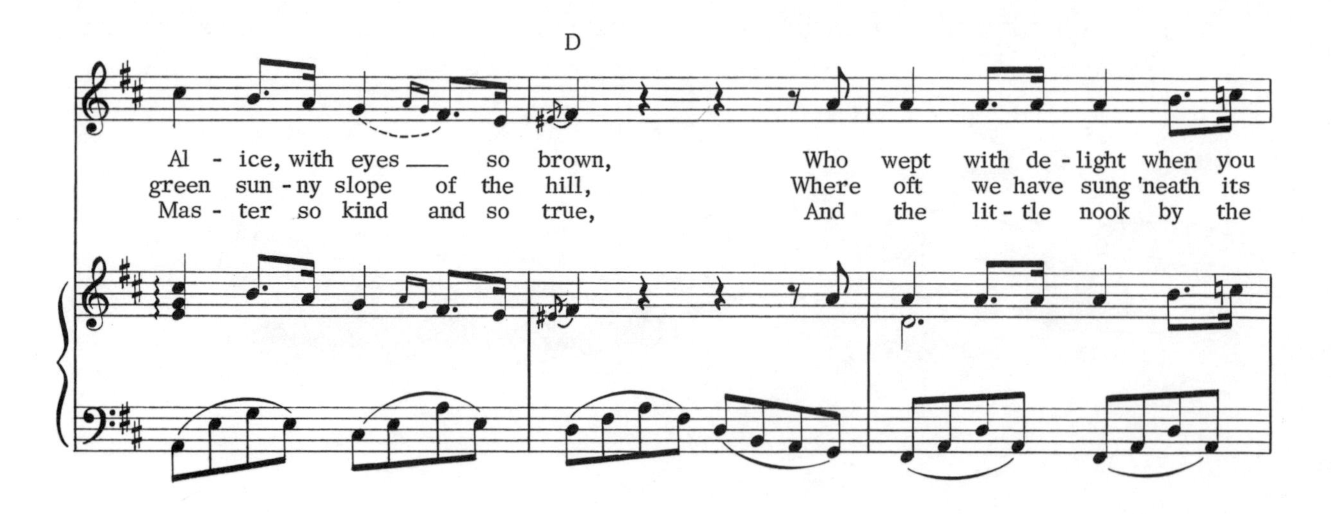

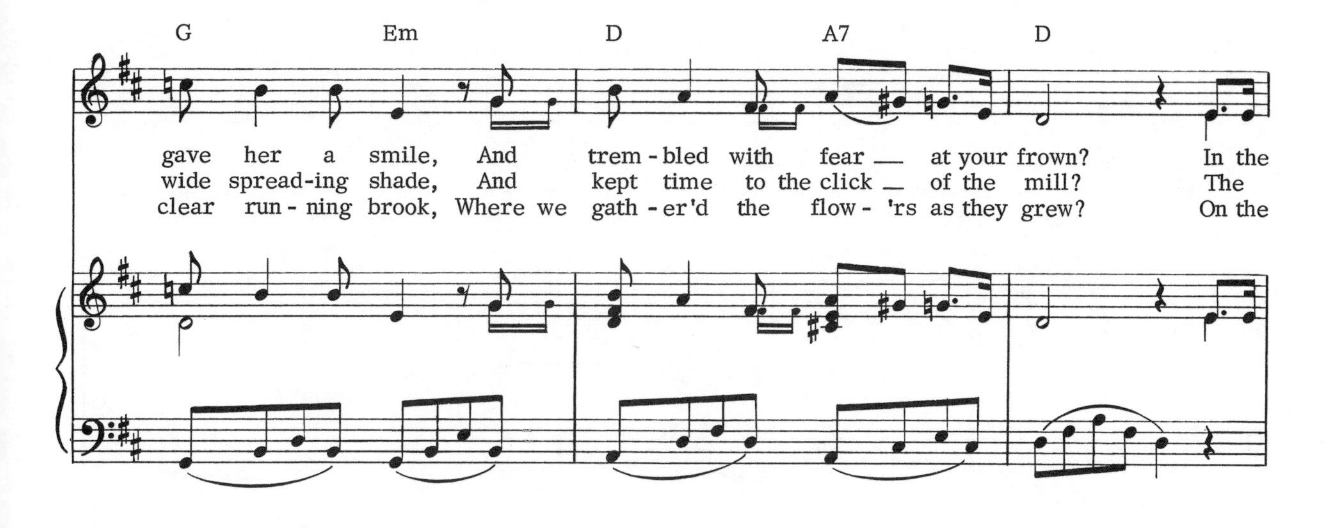
G Em D A7 D
gave her a smile, And trem-bled with fear — at your frown? In the
wide spread-ing shade, And kept time to the click — of the mill? The
clear run-ning brook, Where we gath-er'd the flow-'rs as they grew? On the

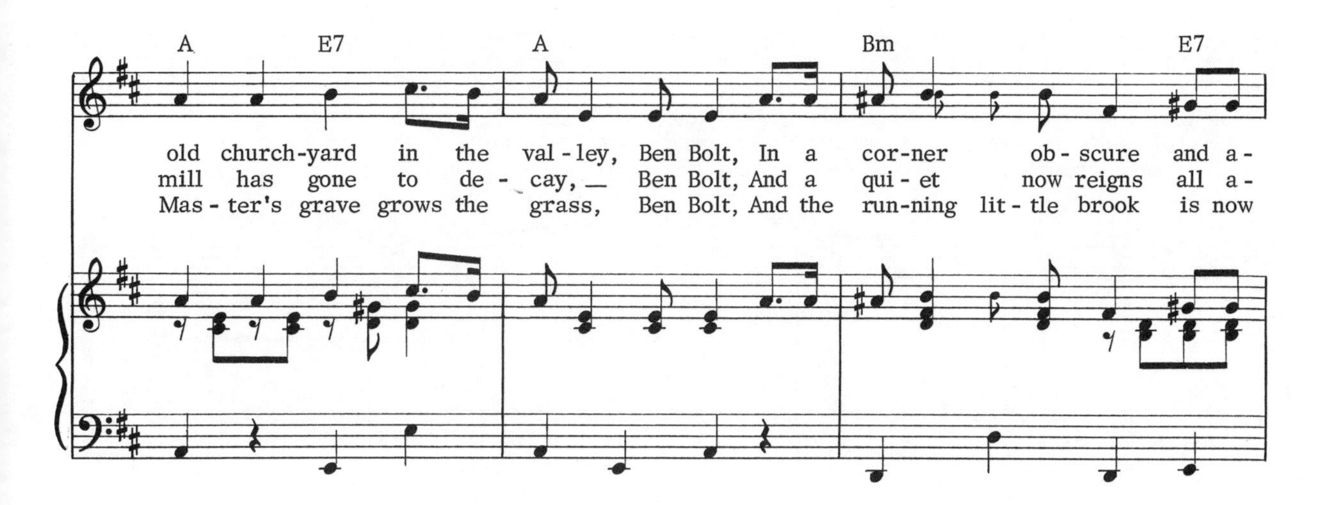
A E7 A Bm E7
old church-yard in the val-ley, Ben Bolt, In a cor-ner ob-scure and a-
mill has gone to de-cay, — Ben Bolt, And a qui-et now reigns all a-
Mas-ter's grave grows the grass, Ben Bolt, And the run-ning lit-tle brook is now

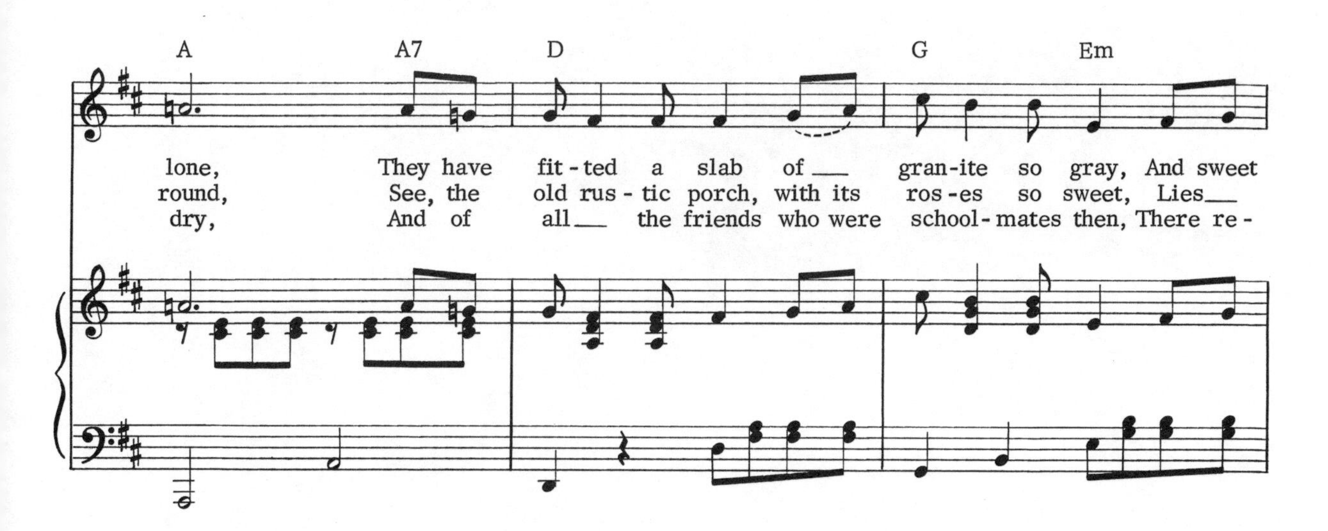
A A7 D G Em
lone, They have fit-ted a slab of — gran-ite so gray, And sweet
round, See, the old rus-tic porch, with its ros-es so sweet, Lies —
dry, And of all — the friends who were school-mates then, There re-

D A7 D A7 D
Al - ice lies un - der the stone; They have fit-ted a slab of —
scat-ter'd and fal-len to the ground; See, the old rus - tic porch, with its
mains, Ben, but you — and — I. And of all — the friends who were
G Em D A7 D G D
gran-ite so gray, And sweet Al - ice lies un - der the stone.
ros - es so sweet, Lies — scat - ter'd and fal - len to the ground.
school - mates then, There re - mains, Ben, but you — and — I.

Keep the Horseshoe over the Door

Words and Music by J. P. Skelly 1880

Skelly, a plumber by trade, also wrote popular songs of many types.
Over the door of the brand-new claim shanty Pa hung his rifle and a bright new horseshoe. Later when he sang about the good luck this would bring, Ma said: "It sounds rather heathenish to me, Charles." SSL, *page 284*

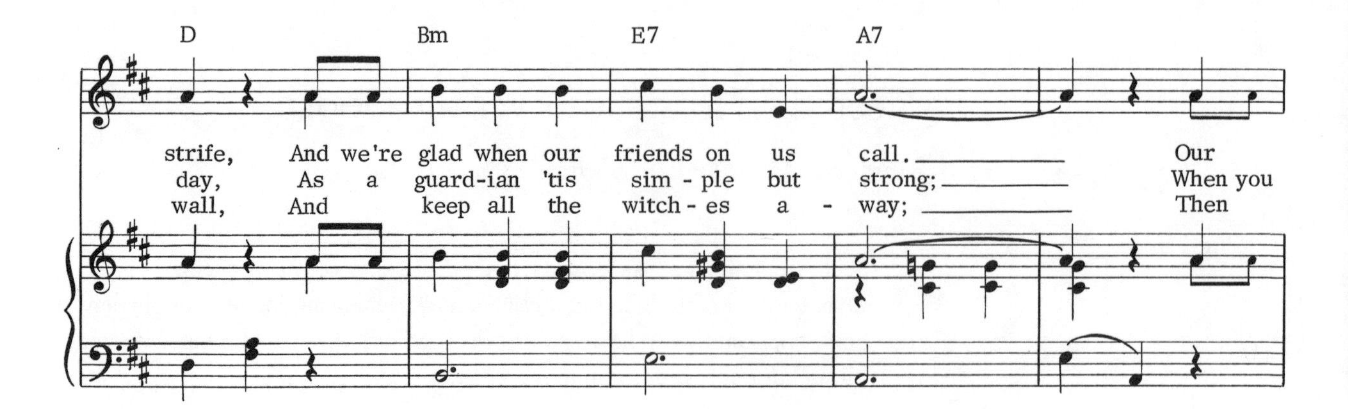
D Bm E7 A7
strife, And we're glad when our friends on us call. Our
day, As a guard-ian 'tis sim - ple but strong; When you
wall, And keep all the witch - es a - way; Then

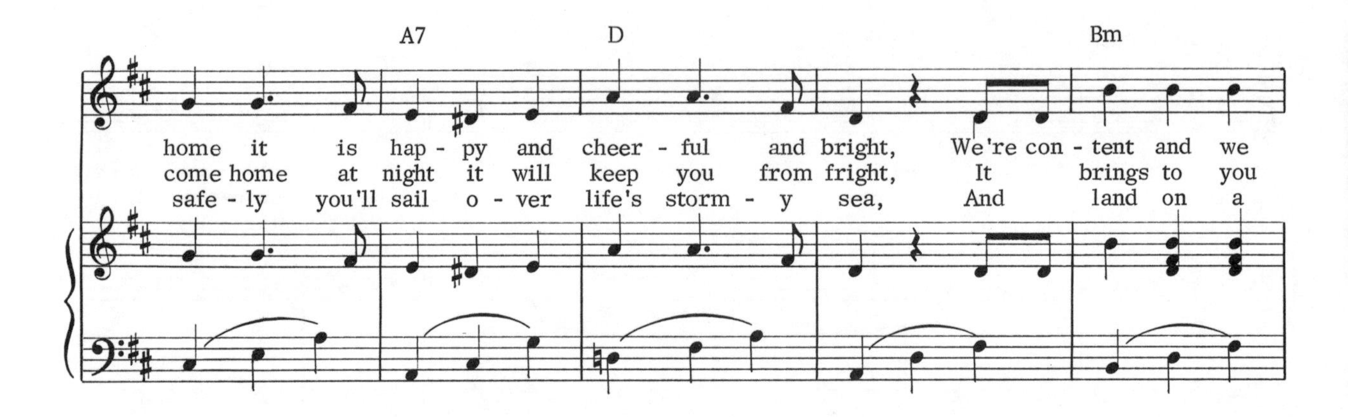
A7 D Bm
home it is hap - py and cheer - ful and bright, We're con - tent and we
come home at night it will keep you from fright, It brings to you
safe - ly you'll sail o - ver life's storm - y sea, And land on a

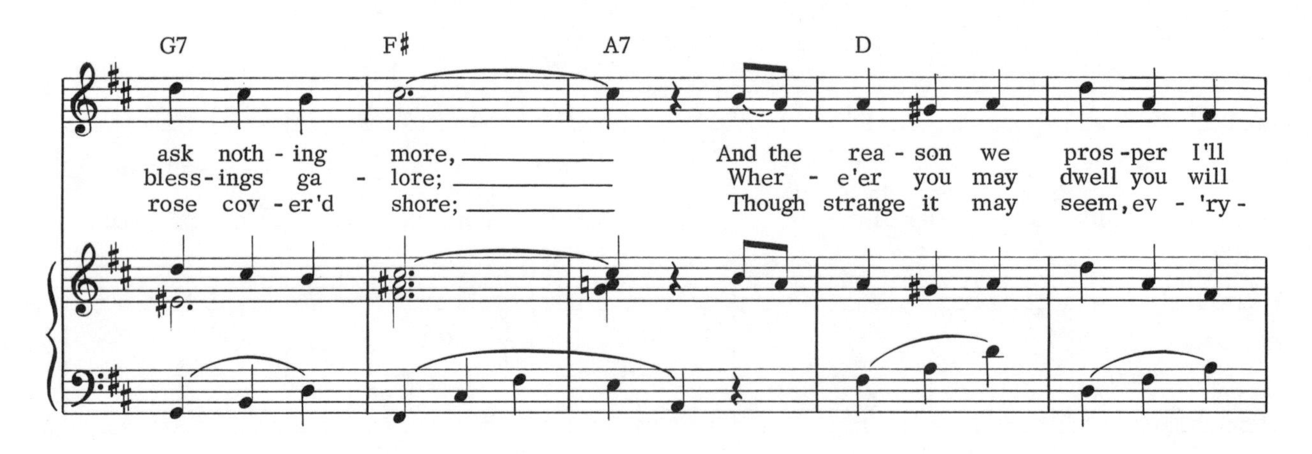
G7 F# A7 D
ask noth - ing more, And the rea - son we pros - per I'll
bless - ings ga - lore; Wher - e'er you may dwell you will
rose cov - er'd shore; Though strange it may seem, ev - 'ry -

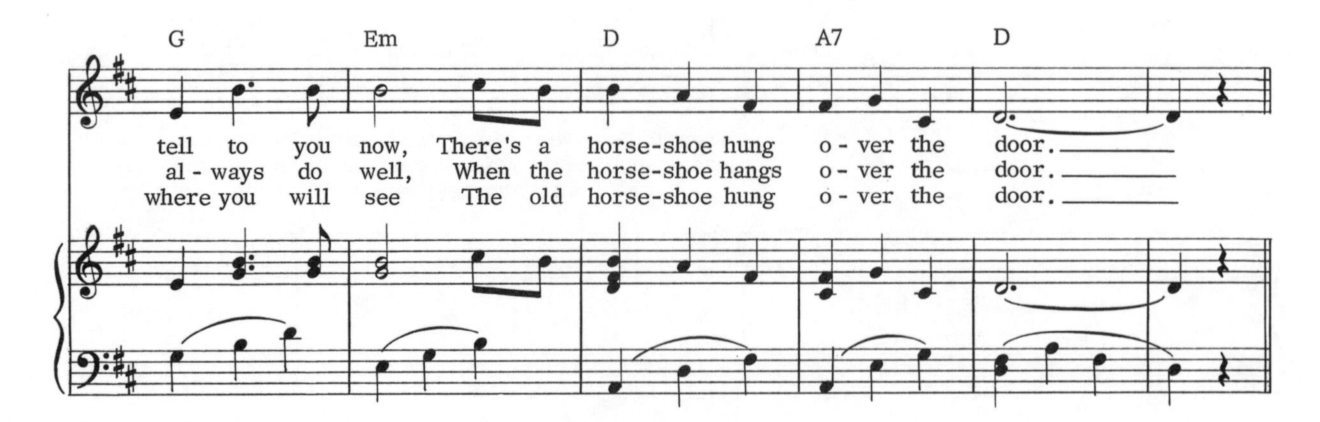
G Em D A7 D
tell to you now, There's a horse - shoe hung o - ver the door.
al - ways do well, When the horse - shoe hangs o - ver the door.
where you will see The old horse - shoe hung o - ver the door.

Chorus
D
A7
Keep the horse-shoe hung o - ver the door, It will bring you good

D
luck ev - er - more; If you want to be hap - py and

G
Em
D
A7
D
free from all care, Keep the horse-shoe hung o - ver the door.

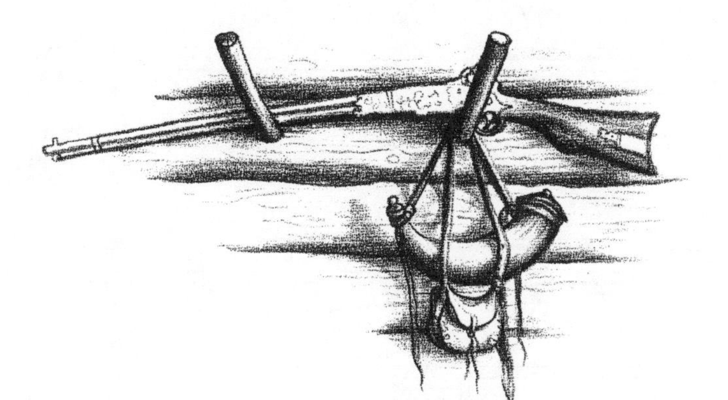

Life Let Us Cherish

Words and Music by Hans Georg Nägeli 1796

Early sheet music attributes this to Mozart; however, it is actually the work of Hans Georg Nägeli, a Swiss music educator and publisher.
When grasshoppers ate the crops so that Pa had to walk back East to get a job, this was the last song he played before putting away the fiddle. BPC, *page 211*

3. The genial seasons soon are o'er,
   Then let us ere we quit this shore
   Contentment seek; it is life's zest,
   The sunshine of the breast.

   (Chorus)

4. Away with every toil and care,
   And cease the rankling thorn to wear,
   With manful hearts life's conflict meet
   Till death sounds the retreat.

   (Chorus)

Oft in the Stilly Night

Words by Thomas Moore   Traditional Scottish Tune   1815

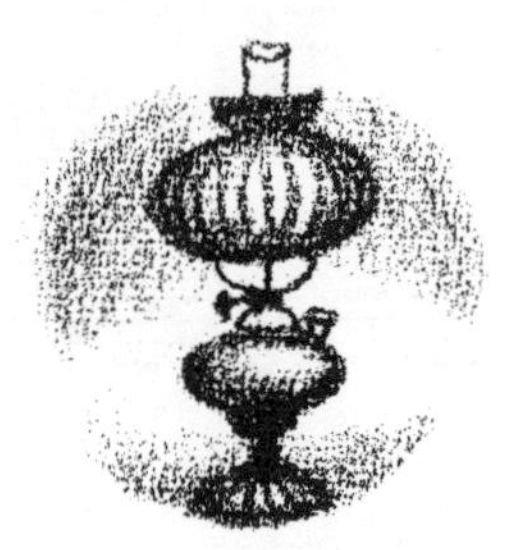

A pensive melody that appeared in Moore's *Selection of Popular National Airs.* This song was one of Abraham Lincoln's favorites.

Toward the end of a lively musical evening, Pa would play some old tunes like this one "to go to sleep on," he said. SSL, *page 213*

D7 G Em Am Em D
boy - hood's years, The words of love then spo - ken; The
treads a - lone Some ban - quet hall de - sert - ed, Whose
G D G A7 D7 G
eyes that shone, now dimmed and gone, The cheer - ful hearts now bro - ken.
lights are fled, whose gar - lands dead, And all but he de - part - ed.
Chorus
G C G D7 G
Thus in the still -y night, Ere slum - ber's chain hath bound me,
G C G D7 G
Sad mem - 'ry brings the light Of oth- er days a - round me.

Rock Me to Sleep

Words by Elizabeth Akers Allen (pseud. Florence Percy)
Music by William Martin 1860

The "Literaries," evening get-togethers of the Literary Society, were started in De Smet to give everybody a good time. There was a different program every Friday, and anyone who could help pitched in. At the musical evening Laura could hardly bear the sadness of this song. All the women were wiping their eyes, and the men were clearing their throats. LTP, *page 223*

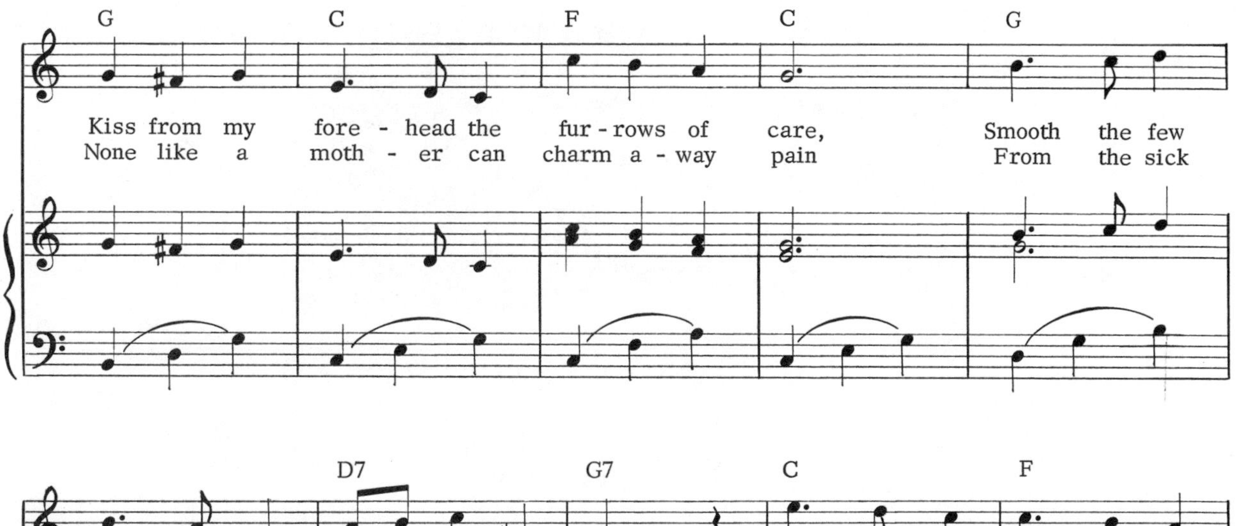

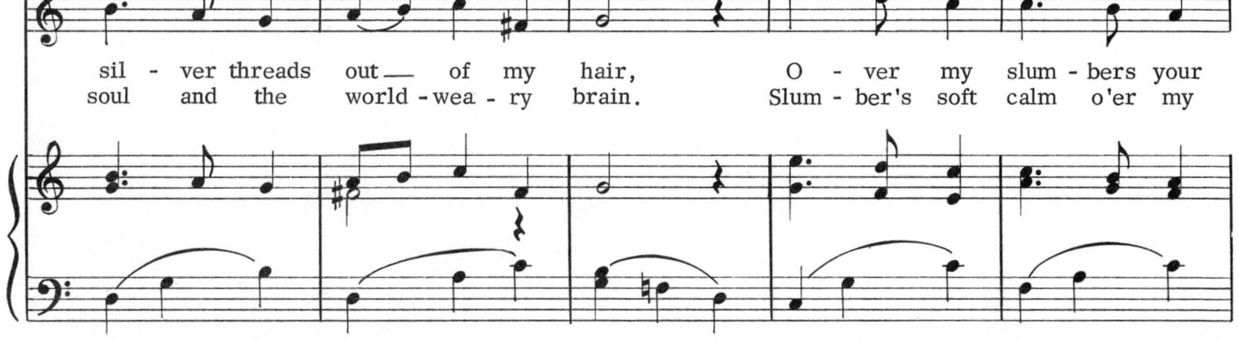

3. Mother, dear mother, the years have been long
Since I last hushed to your lullaby song;
Sing then and unto my soul it shall seem
Womanhood's years have been only a dream.
Clasped to your heart in a loving embrace,
With your light lashes just sweeping my face,
Never hereafter to wake or to weep;
Rock me to sleep, mother, rock me to sleep!

Love's Old Sweet Song

Words by Clifton Bingham   Music by James L. Molloy   1884

James Lyman Molloy, an Irish lawyer, was also well-known as a composer. This is the most famous of his songs.

The evening before Laura's wedding Pa played all the old tunes that she had known ever since she could remember and finished with "Just a song at twilight. . . ." HGY, *page 277*

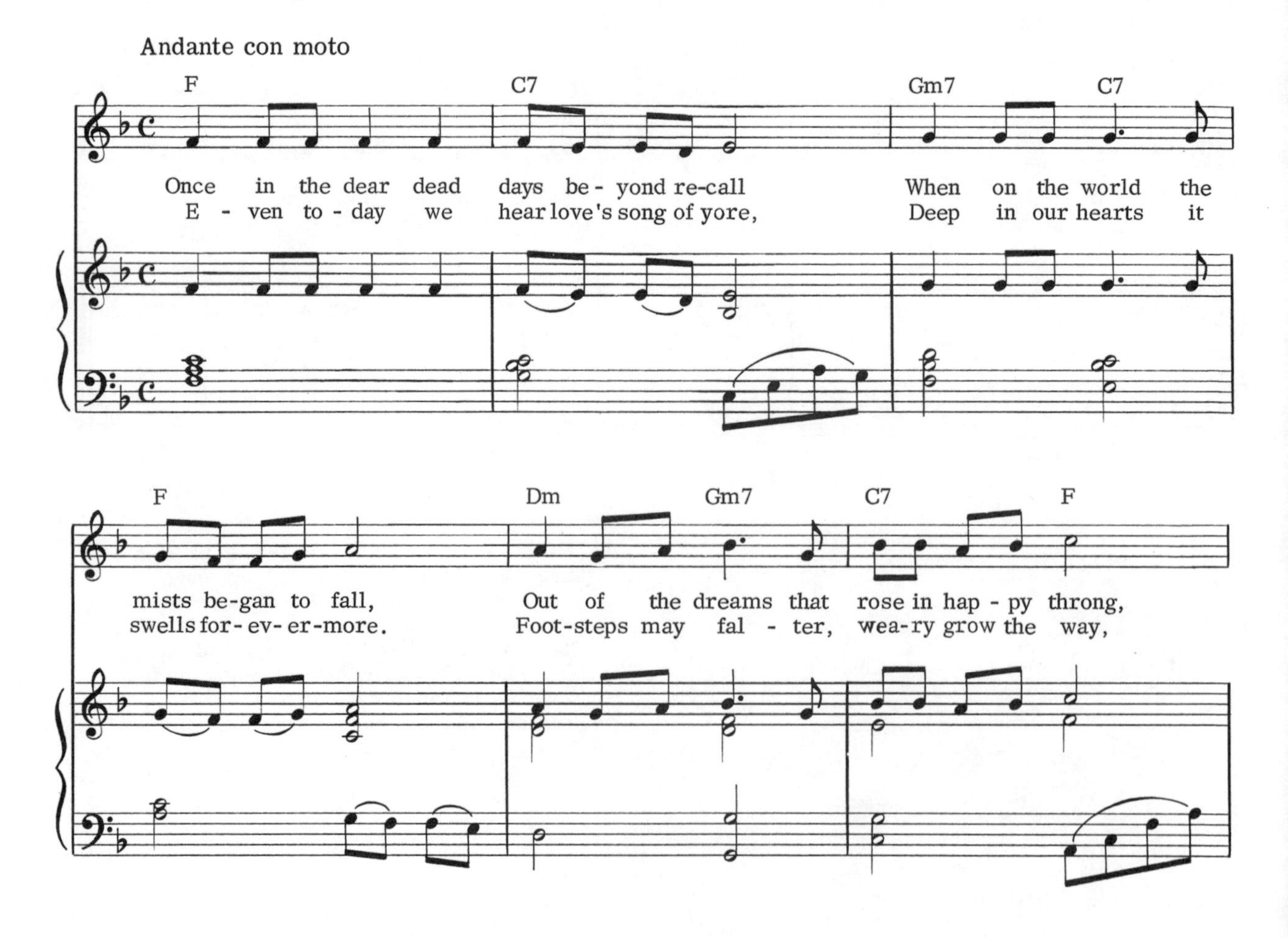

Dm7 G7 C C9
Low to our hearts love sang an old sweet song. And in the dusk where
Still we can hear it at the close of day. So to the end when
F G7 Am Dm C G7 C7
fell the fire-light gleam Soft-ly it wove it-self in-to our dream.
life's dim shad-ows fall, Love will be found the sweet-est song of all.
Chorus
F C7
Just a song at twi-light, when the lights are
F A7 Dm G7
low And the flick-'ring shad-ows soft-ly come and

C7
F
C7
Gm6
go,
Though the heart be
wea - ry,
sad the day and

A7
F7
B♭
F
C7
long,
Still to us at
twi - light
comes love's old

F
B♭
F
C7
F
B♭
F
song,
Comes
love's
old
sweet
song.

Favorites of Long Ago

Buy a Broom

Words Anonymous   Traditional Austrian Tune   Circa 1830

This nursery favorite was originally popular with adults; an early presentation at the Park Theatre in New York met with "the most Unbounded Approbation." It was a song that Laura loved when she learned it from her Cousin Lena in the railroad camp at Silver Lake. SSL, *page 94*

2. To brush off the insects that come to annoy you
   You'll find it quite useful by night and by day,
   And what better exercise, pray can employ you,
   Than to sweep all vexatious intruders away?
      Buy a broom, buy a broom!
      Than to sweep all vexatious intruders away?

3. Ere winter comes on for sweet home soon departing
   My toils for your favor again I'll resume,
   And while gratitude's tear in my eyelid is starting,
   Bless the time that in England I cried buy a broom!
      Buy a broom, buy a broom!
      Bless the time that in England I cried buy a broom!

Camptown Races

Words and Music by Stephen Foster 1850

Many of Stephen Foster's melodies are reminiscent of Negro folk music; the chorus of "Camptown Races" is similar to "Roll, Jordan, Roll."

The music would go rollicking while Pa and Mr. Boast sang: "I bet my money on the bob-tailed mare!" Ma did not approve of gambling, but her toe could not stop tapping to this tune. SSL, *page 212*

3. Old muley cow come onto the track, Doo-dah! doo-dah!
The bobtail fling her over her back, Oh! doo-dah-day!
Then fly along like a railroad car, Doo-dah! doo-dah!
Running a race with a shooting star, Oh! doo-dah-day!

(Chorus)

4. See them flying on a ten-mile heat, Doo-dah! doo-dah!
Round the racetrack, then repeat, Oh! doo-dah-day!
I win my money on the bobtailed mare, Doo-dah! doo-dah!
I keep my money in an old tow bag, Oh! doo-dah-day!

(Chorus)

Golden Years Are Passing By

Words and Music by Will L. Thompson 1879

Will L. Thompson was a prolific nineteenth-century song writer whose sentimental ballads enjoyed great popularity.

The family sat in the deepening dusk. The land flattened to blackness, and in the clear air above it the stars hung low. Then Pa said: "Here is one for you girls." Softly he sang; the music drifted away and was gone. HGY, *page 156*

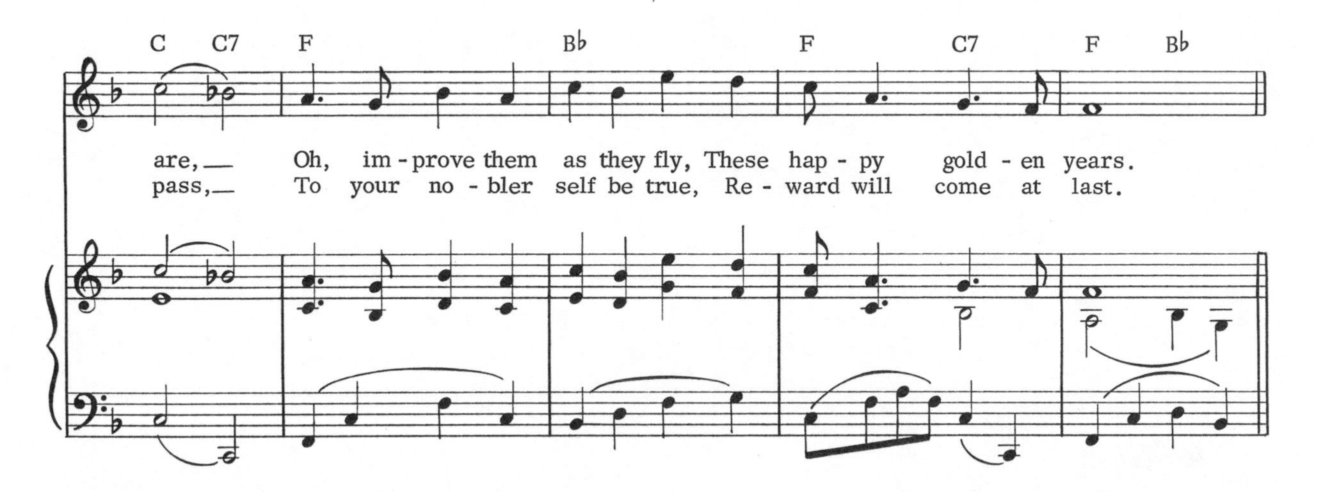

Chorus

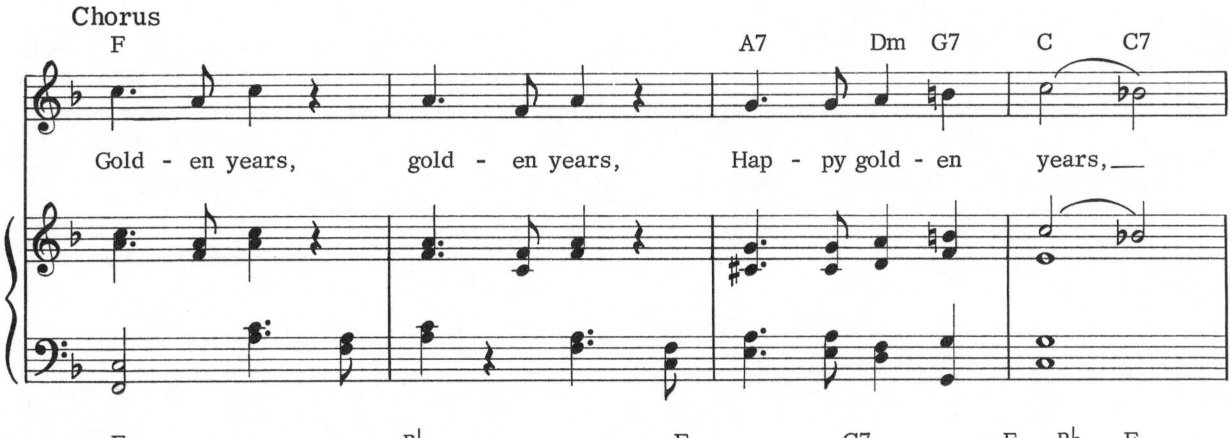

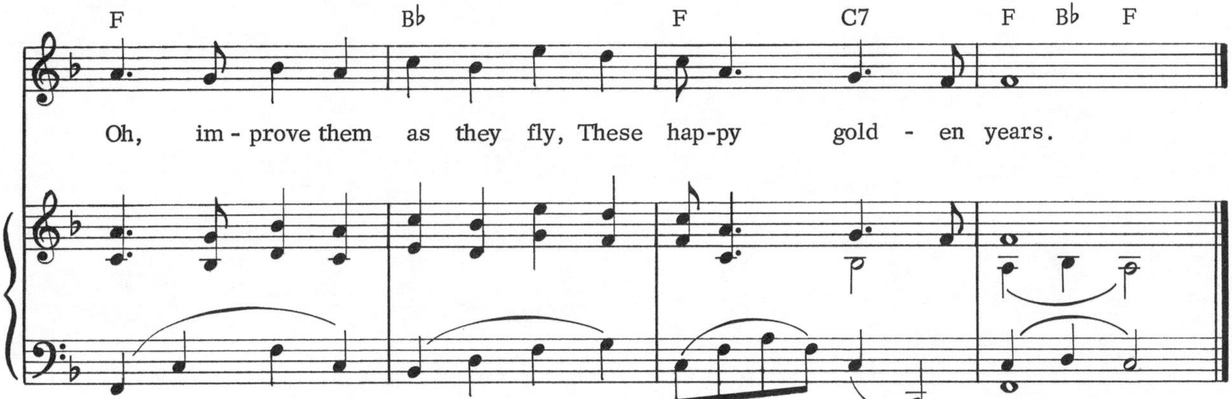

3. Golden years are passing by,
Fleeting, fleeting swiftly on,
Life is but a passing hour,
Before we know 'tis gone;
Soon the parting time will come,
Day by day it nears.
Have you done your duty well,
These happy golden years?

(Chorus)

Paddle Your Own Canoe

Words and Music by Harry Clifton 1867

This is one of the moralizing songs, based on homely maxims, that were highly esteemed during the late nineteenth century.

Comfortably settled in at Silver Lake's deserted railroad camp forty miles away from the nearest neighbors, Pa said: "Now here's something worth singing. It's what we'll be doing this winter." SSL, *page 148*

G D7 G D
pad - dle my own ca - noe. My wants are few, I
pad - dle your own ca - noe. To "bor-row" is dear - er by
A7 D
care not at all If my debts are paid when due. I
far than to "buy," A max - im tho' old still true; You
A7 D
drive a - way strife in the o-cean of life While I pad - dle my own ca - noe.
nev-er will sigh if you on - ly will try To pad - dle your own ca - noe.
Chorus
G D7 G C
Then love your neigh - bor as your - self, As the

3. If a hurricane rise in the midday skies,
And the sun is lost to view;
Move steadily by with a steadfast eye,
And paddle your own canoe;
The daisies that grow in the bright green fields
Are blooming so sweet for you,
So never sit down, with a tear or a frown,
But paddle your own canoe.

(Chorus)

It Will Never Do to Give It Up So

Words and Music by Daniel Decatur Emmett 1843

This was one of Daniel Emmett's early minstrel successes. The chorus shows the influence of Irish and Scottish reels.

During one of the long winter's savage blizzards when Pa's hands were too cracked and stiff to play the fiddle, he led the family in singing this spirited ditty about facing up to trouble on "the old Jim River." LW, *page 291*

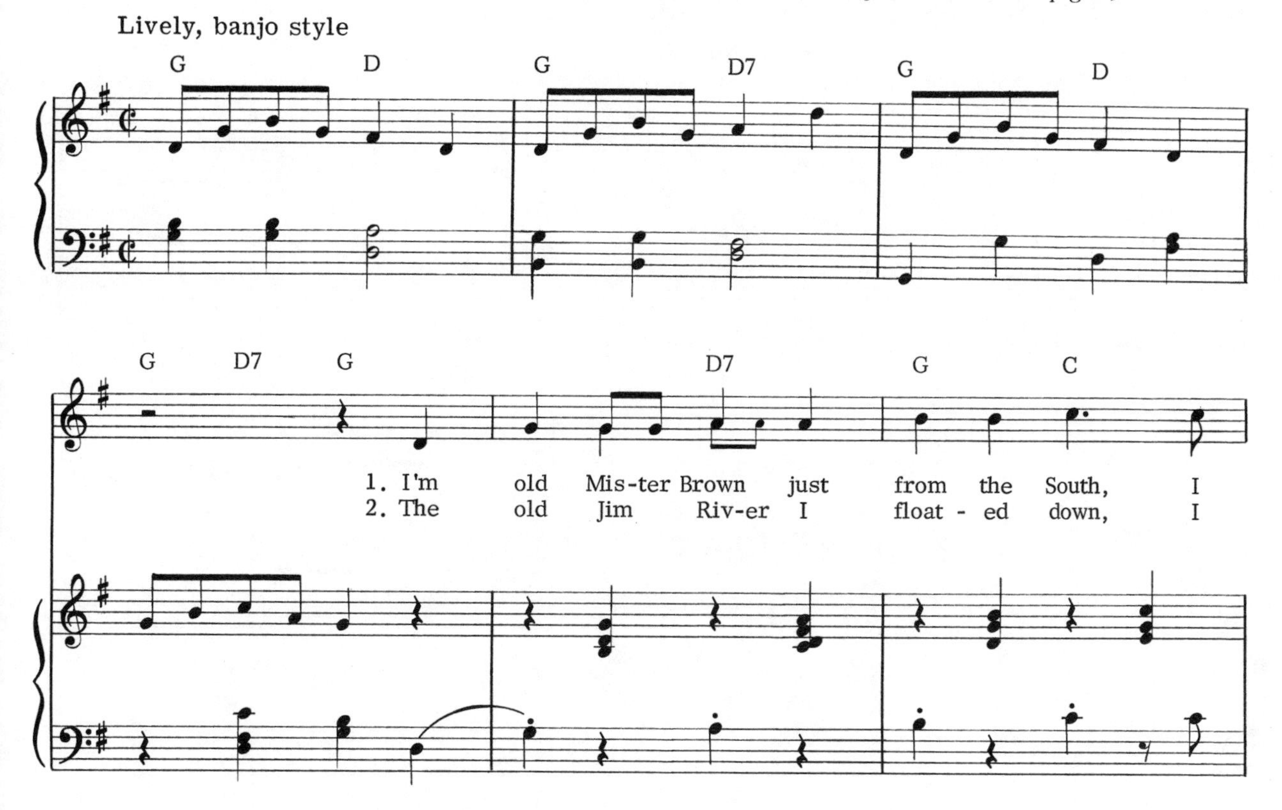

G D7 G D7
left Lynch-burg in the time of the drouth; The times they got so
ran my boat up - on the groun'; The drift log come with a
G C G D7 G D7
bad in the place That we poor folks dared not show our face.
rush-ing din And stove both ends of my old boat in.
Chorus
G D7
It will nev-er do to give it up so, It will
G D7
nev-er do to give it up so, It will nev-er do to give it up

3. The old log rake me aft and fore,
   It left my cookhouse on the shore;
   I thought it wouldn't do to give it up so
   So I scull myself ashore with the old banjo.

   (Chorus)

4. I gets on shore and feels very glad,
   I looks at the banjo and feels very mad;
   I walks up the bank that's slick as glass,
   Up went my heels and I light upon the grass.

   (Chorus)

5. By golly, but it surely made me laugh,
   With my boat I made a raft;
   I had a pine tree for a sail
   And steered her down with my coattail.

   (Chorus)

6. That same night as the sun did set,
   I 'rived in town with my clothes all wet;
   Then I built up a great big fire,
   If that's not true then I am a liar.

   (Chorus)

Oh, Susanna

Words Traditional USA, California Gold Rush Version
Music by Stephen Foster 1848

This parody of Stephen Foster's minstrel ditty was called "The California Immigrant"; it was first heard at the farewell banquet for a young man who was leaving for California on the sailing ship *Eliza*. The new version became the theme song of the forty-niners and later pioneers.

Pa often sang it beside his prairie campfire. LHP, *page 333*

2. I jumped aboard the *'Liza* ship
   And traveled on the sea,
   And every time I thought of home,
   I wished it wasn't me!
   The vessel reared like any horse,
   That had of oats a wealth,
   I found it wouldn't throw me so
   I thought I'd throw myself!

   (Chorus)

3. I thought of all the pleasant times
   We've had together here,
   I thought I ought to cry a bit,
   But couldn't find a tear.
   The pilot's bread* was in my mouth,
   The gold dust in my eye,
   And though I'm going far away,
   Dear brothers, don't you cry!

   *(hard tack)

   (Chorus)

4. I soon shall be in Frisco
   And there I'll look around,
   And when I see the gold lumps there,
   I'll pick them off the ground.
   I'll scrape the mountains clean, my boys,
   I'll drain the rivers dry,
   A pocketful of rocks bring home,
   So brothers, don't you cry!

   (Chorus)

The Campbells Are Coming

Words and Music Traditional Scottish Circa 1715

The evening before starting his three-hundred-mile walk to get work, Pa played for a long time in the twilight. This stirring march was one of the tunes. When bedtime came, he said: "Take good care of the old fiddle, Caroline. It puts heart into a man." BPC, *page 211*

3. The Campbells they are a' in arms;
 Their loyal faith and truth to show;
 Wi' banners rattling in the wind,
 The Campbells are coming, Hurrah! Hurrah!

(Chorus)

All the Blue Bonnets Are over the Border

Words by Sir Walter Scott   Traditional Scottish Tune   Circa 1820

The "Border Ballad" from Scott's *Monastery*, set to an ancient Scottish air, became widely popular in the United States during the early nineteenth century. Its rousing strains helped to ease the rigors of the long winter. Pa said: "Blamed if that old tune don't give me the spunk to like fighting even a blizzard!" LW, *page 43*

3. Trumpets are sounding, war steeds are bounding,
Stand to your arms and march in good order;
England shall many a day tell of the bloody fray,
When the blue bonnets came over the border.

(Chorus)

Where There's a Will There's a Way

Words and Music by Harry Clifton 1867

The hard winter was over; the train had come at last with food. The Ingalls family and their friends the Boasts celebrated springtime by having the Christmas dinner they had all gone without. Afterwards everyone joined in this new song, and as they sang fear and suffering seemed to rise like a dark cloud and float away on the music. LW, *page 334*

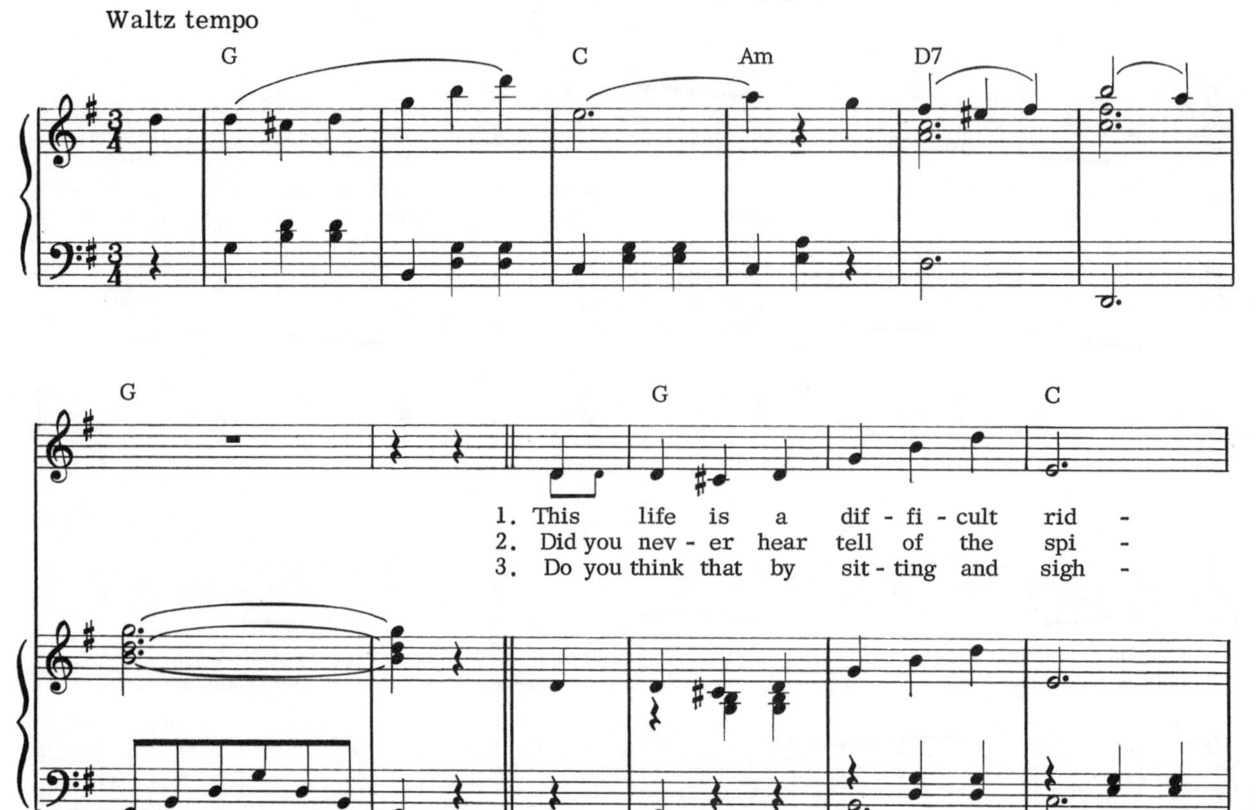

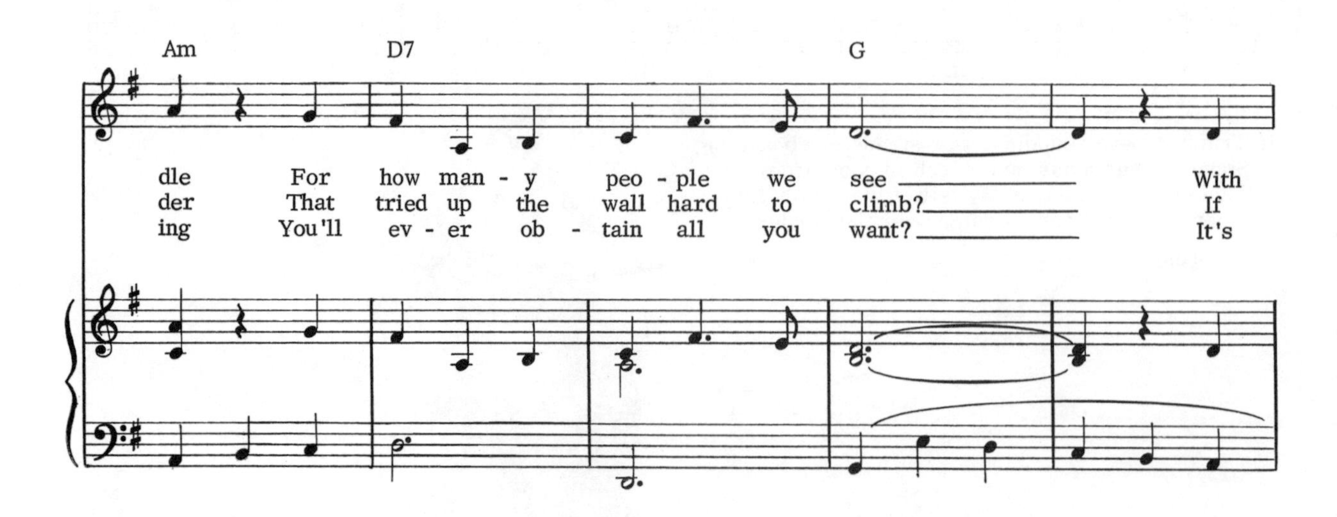

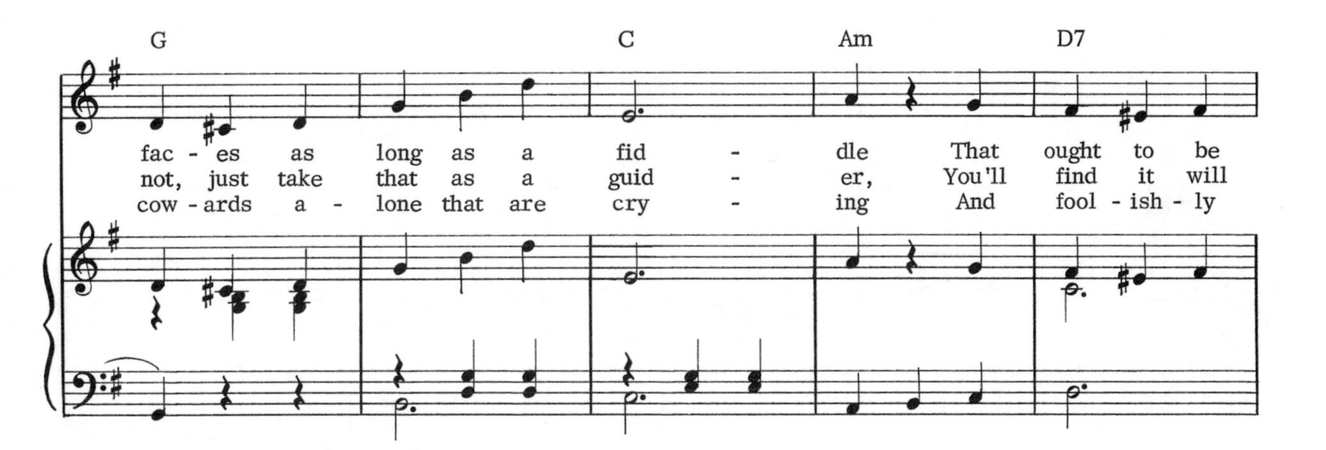
G C Am D7
fac - es as long as a fid - dle That ought to be
not, just take that as a guid - er, You'll find it will
cow - ards a - lone that are cry - ing And fool - ish - ly

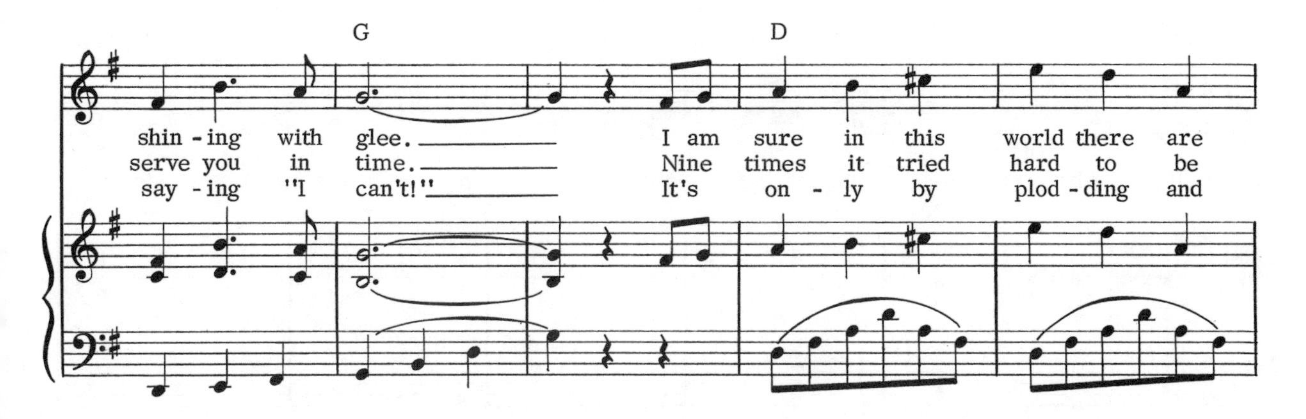
G D
shin - ing with glee. I am sure in this world there are
serve you in time. Nine times it tried hard to be
say - ing "I can't!" It's on - ly by plod - ding and

Em A D
plen - ty Of good things e - nough for us all.
mount - ing And ev - 'ry time it stuck fast.
striv - ing And la - bor - ing up the steep hill,

Em
And yet there's not one out of twen -
But it tried hard a - gain with - out count -
Of life that you'll ev - er be thriv -

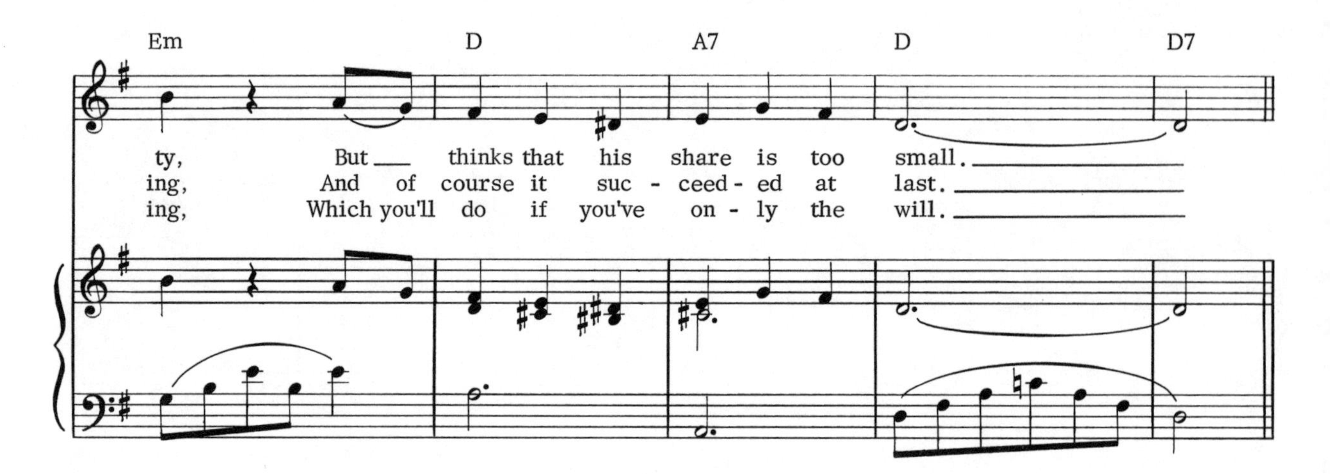
Em D A7 D D7
ty, But thinks that his share is too small.
ing, And of course it suc - ceed - ed at last.
ing, Which you'll do if you've on - ly the will.

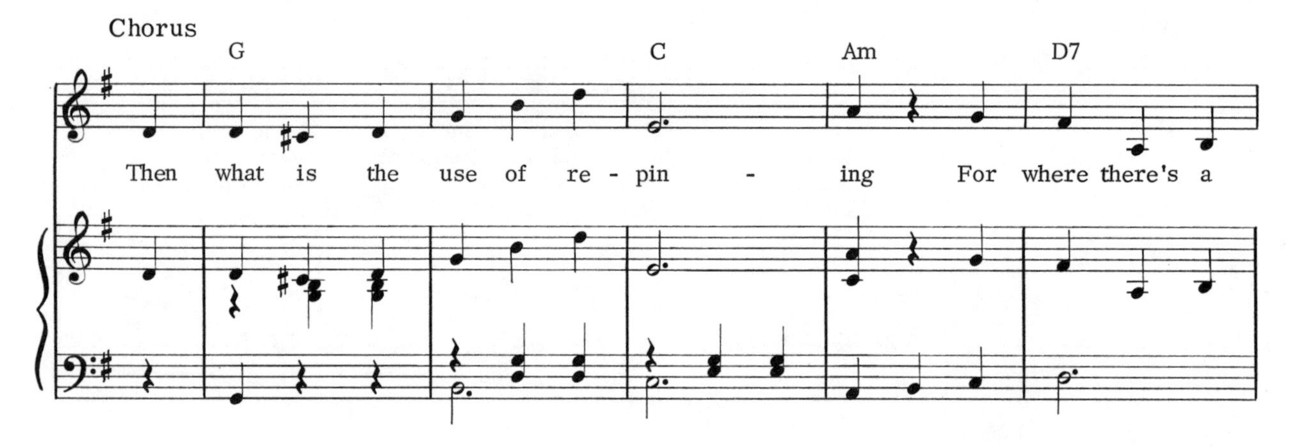
Chorus
G C Am D7
Then what is the use of re - pin - ing For where there's a

G
will there's a way, And to - mor - row the sun may be

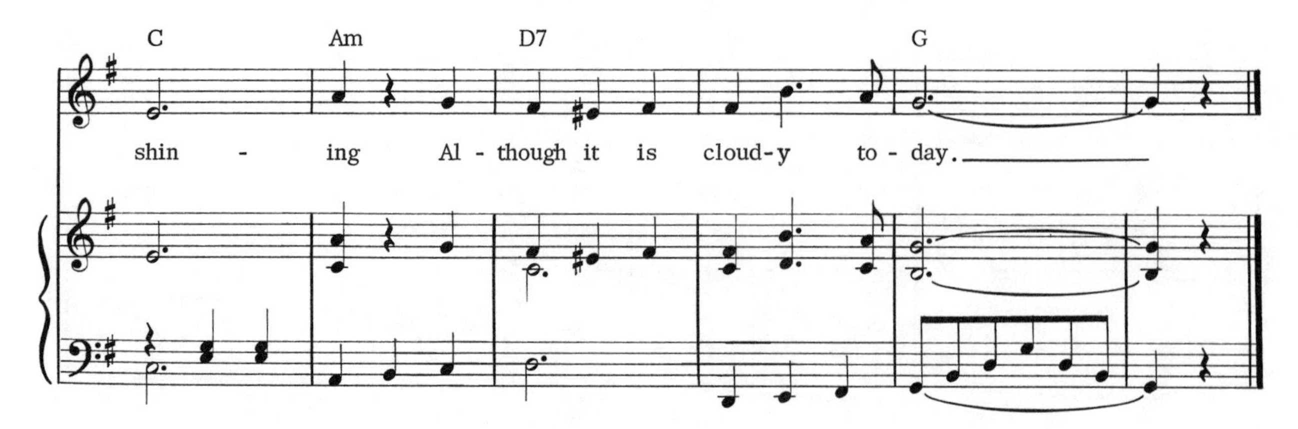
C Am D7 G
shin - ing Al - though it is cloud - y to - day.

Ballads, Games, and Dances

Billy Boy

Words and Music Traditional USA

This folk song is a nonsense version of the grim classic ballad "Lord Randal." The happy winter evenings had begun at Silver Lake. Gaily, Pa played and sang: "She can make a cherry pie, charming Billy." His eyes twinkled at Ma while the music laughed and whirled. SSL, *page 212*

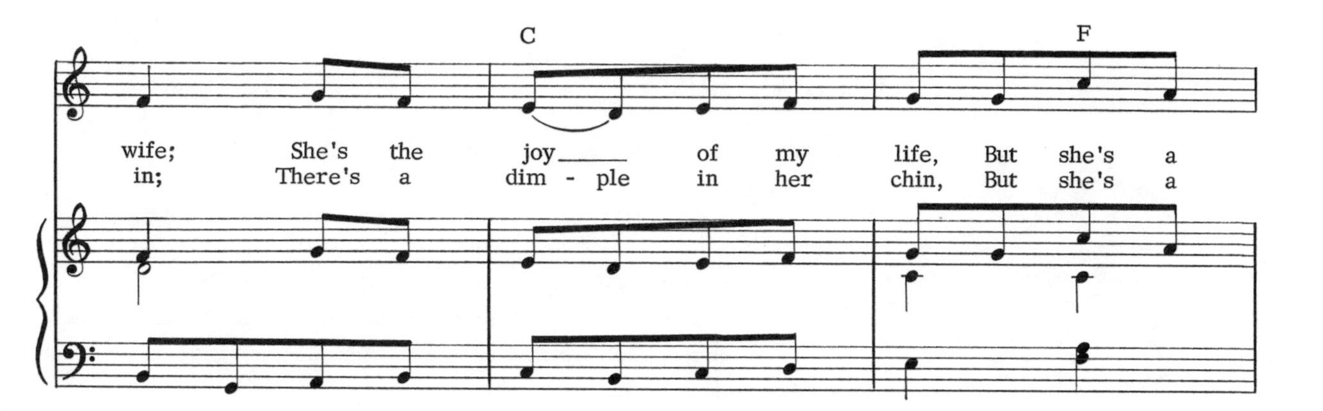

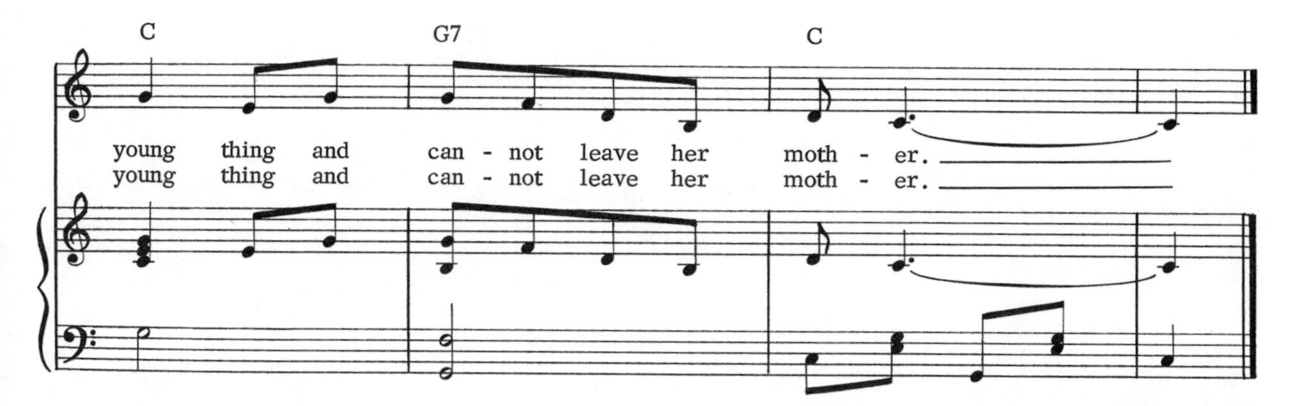

3. Did she set for you a chair, Billy boy, Billy boy;
   Did she set for you a chair, charming Billy?
   Yes, she set for me a chair;
   She has ringlets in her hair,
   But she's a young thing and cannot leave her mother.

4. Can she make a cherry pie, Billy boy, Billy boy;
   Can she make a cherry pie, charming Billy?
   She can make a cherry pie,
   With a twinkle in her eye,
   But she's a young thing and cannot leave her mother.

5. Is she often seen at church, Billy boy, Billy boy;
   Is she often seen at church, charming Billy?
   Yes, she's often seen at church,
   With a bonnet white as birch,
   But she's a young thing and cannot leave her mother.

6. How tall is she, Billy boy, Billy boy;
   How tall is she, charming Billy?
   She's as tall as any pine,
   And as straight as a pumpkin vine,
   But she's a young thing and cannot leave her mother.

7. Are her eyes very bright, Billy boy, Billy boy;
   Are her eyes very bright, charming Billy?
   Yes, her eyes are very bright,
   But, alas, they're minus sight,
   But she's a young thing and cannot leave her mother.

8. How old is she, Billy boy, Billy boy;
   How old is she, charming Billy?
   She is four times seven,
   Twenty-eight and eleven,
   But she's a young thing and cannot leave her mother.

Buffalo Gals

Originally called "Lubly Fan," this minstrel-show number and play-party song underwent various changes of name to fit different localities. When the fiddle sang it at Grandpa's dance and Pa called "Swing your partners," skirts swirled and boots stamped and partners bowed and separated and met and bowed again. LHBW, *page 145*

A7
D
chanced to meet, Oh! She was fair to view.
whole side - walk As she stood close by me.
all my life If I had her by my side.

Chorus

D
Oh, you Buf - fa - lo gals, will you come out to - night, Will you

A7
D
come out to-night, will you come out to-night, Buf - fa - lo gals, will you

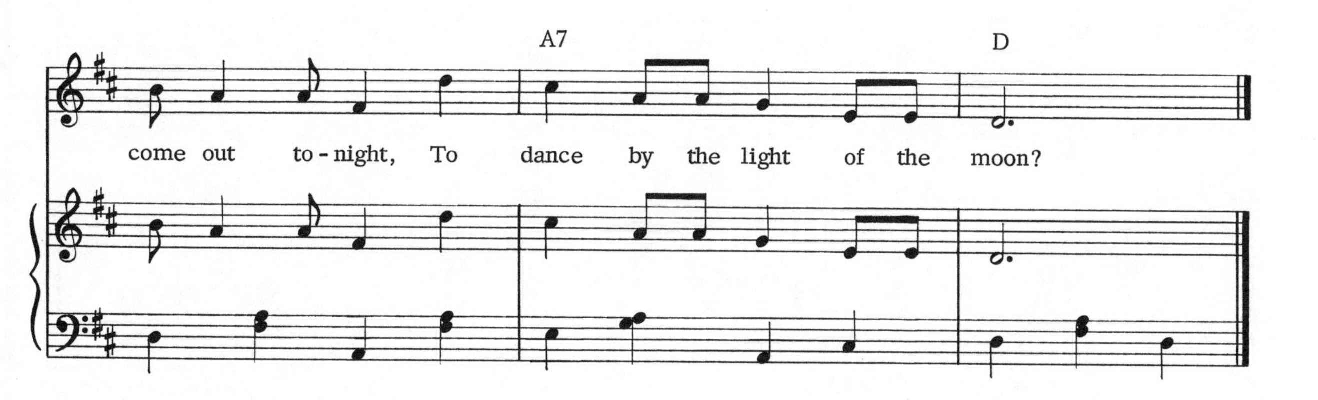
A7
D
come out to-night, To dance by the light of the moon?

The Singing School

Words and Music by P. Benson 1869

Gently satirized in this nonsense song, the singing school was a long-established part of American musical tradition.

Laura loved the singing school and its gay evenings. First the class learned the notes; then they practiced scales, exercises, and songs. At recess everyone talked and laughed together. And on the way home with Almanzo, Laura sang this song again. HGY, *page 212*

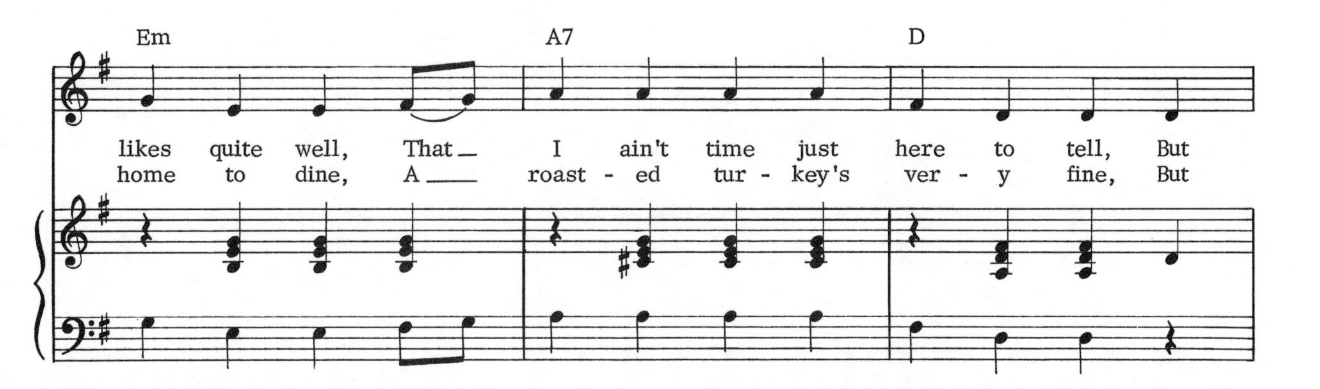
Em
A7
D
likes quite well, That __ I ain't time just here to tell, But
home to dine, A ___ roast - ed tur - key's ver - y fine, But

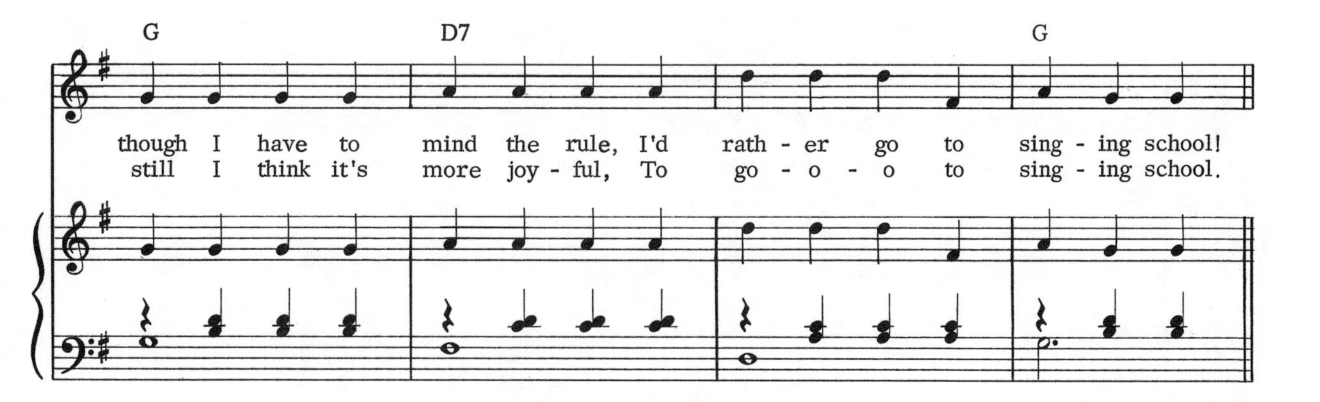
G
D7
G
though I have to mind the rule, I'd rath - er go to sing - ing school!
still I think it's more joy - ful, To go - o - o to sing - ing school.

Chorus
G
C
G
Oh, the sing - ing school's beau - ti - ful, Oh, the

C
Am
D7
G
sing - ing school's beau - ti - ful, If you'll have me for your teach - er, I shall

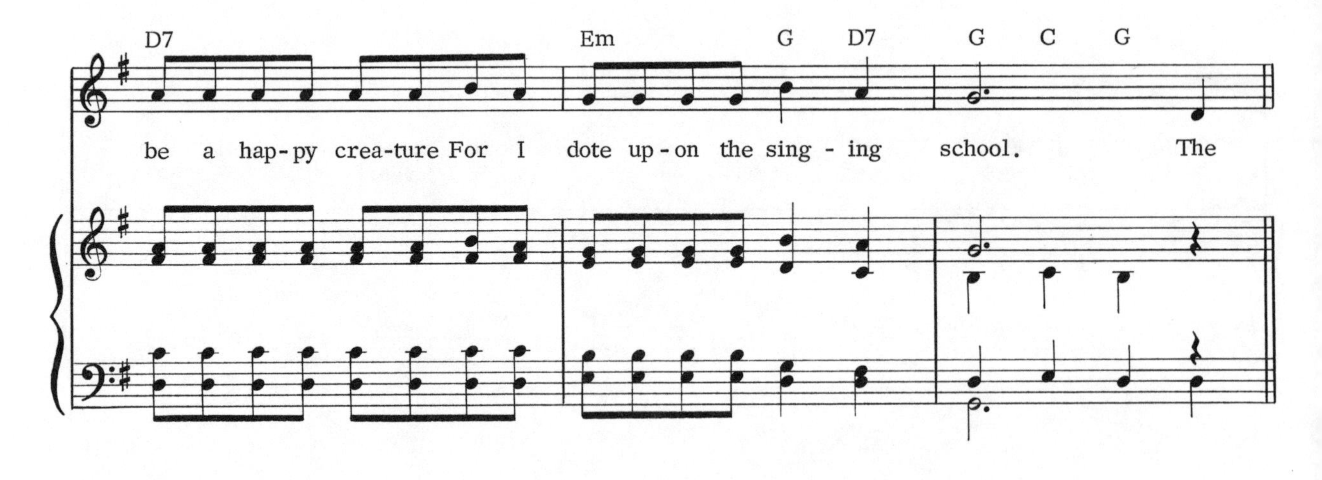

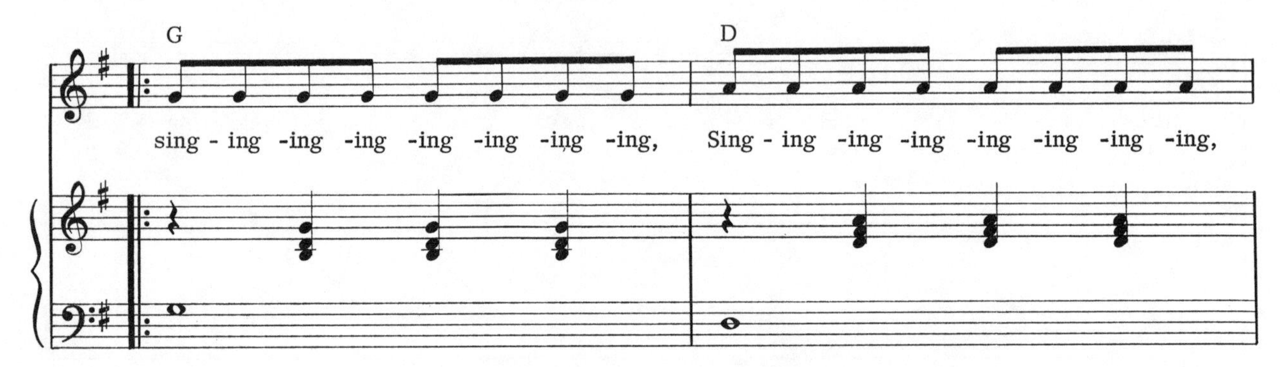

3. Some think that nothing's half so good,
As oysters roasted, fried, or stewed,
And others think the pleasure's more
A-slidin' on a cellar door.
So some think this and some think that,
But all agree there's greater sat-
Isfaction to be always had,
At singing school as I have said.

(Chorus)

4. Oh, sweet the breath of dewy morn,
A-blowin' sadly through the corn,
While golden rays of mystic light
Is heard upon the dawn of night.
But superfine, ecstatic bliss,
You'll always find and never miss,
If you will only mind this rule,
And always go to singing school.

(Chorus)

Captain Jinks

Words by William Horace Lingard   Music by T. Maclagan   1869

This is an English music-hall number that was an instant success when introduced in the United States. The "horse" referred to is not a four-legged one but the troop of marines for whose rations their captain was responsible.

Ma set a pan of beautiful, brown baked beans and a pan of golden corn bread on the table. Then Pa sang: "I'm Captain Jinks. . . ." BPC, *page 338*

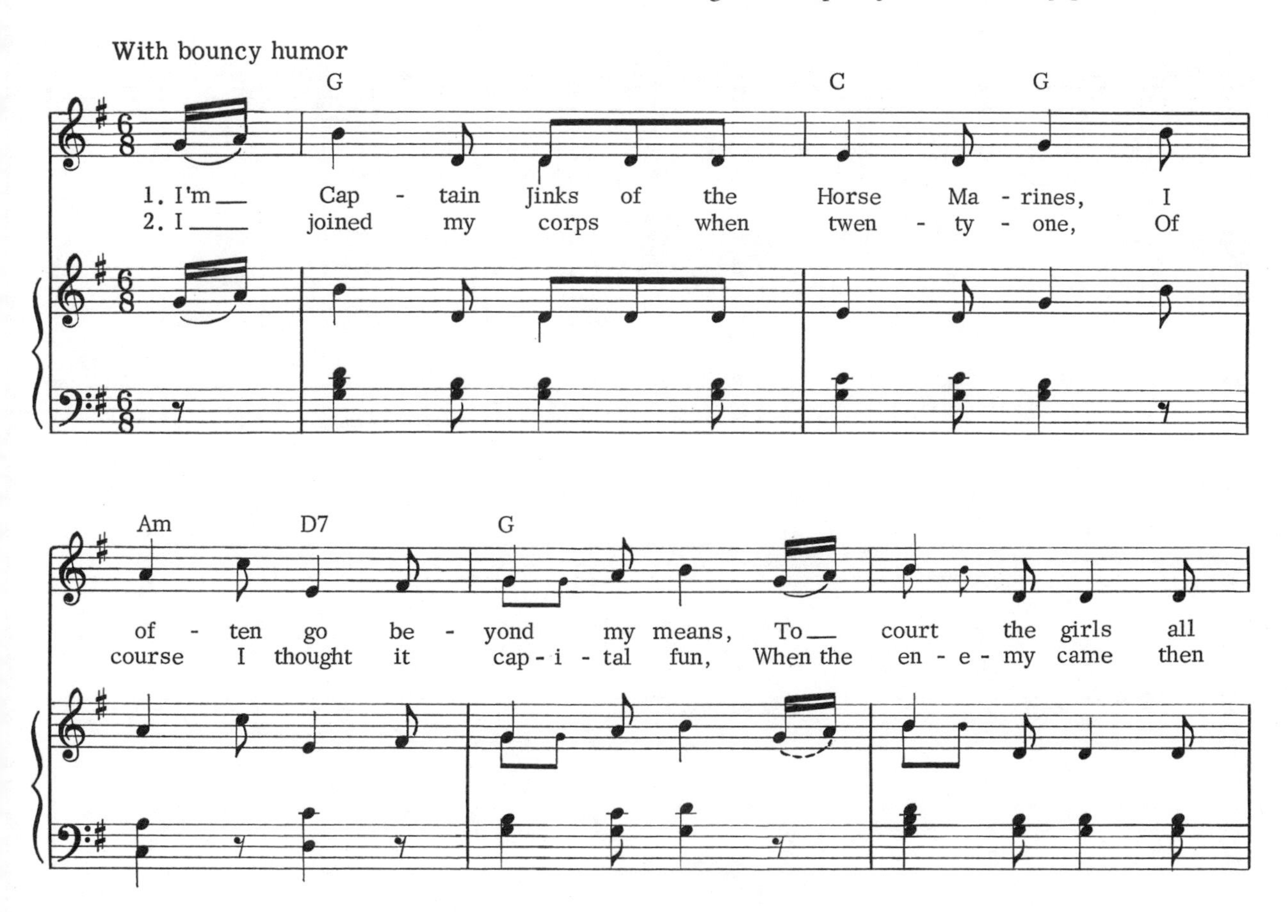

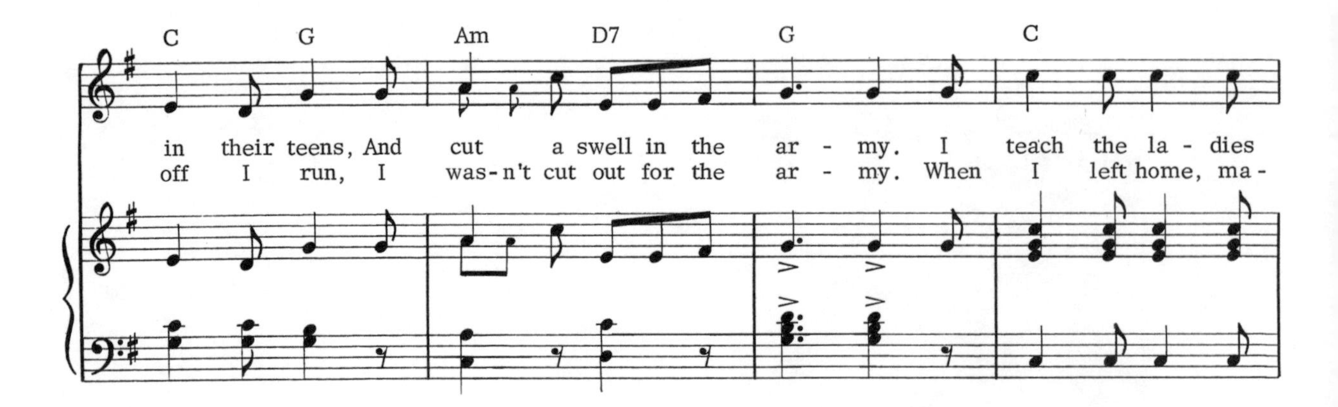
C G Am D7 G C
in their teens, And cut a swell in the ar - my. I teach the la - dies
off I run, I was-n't cut out for the ar - my. When I left home, ma -

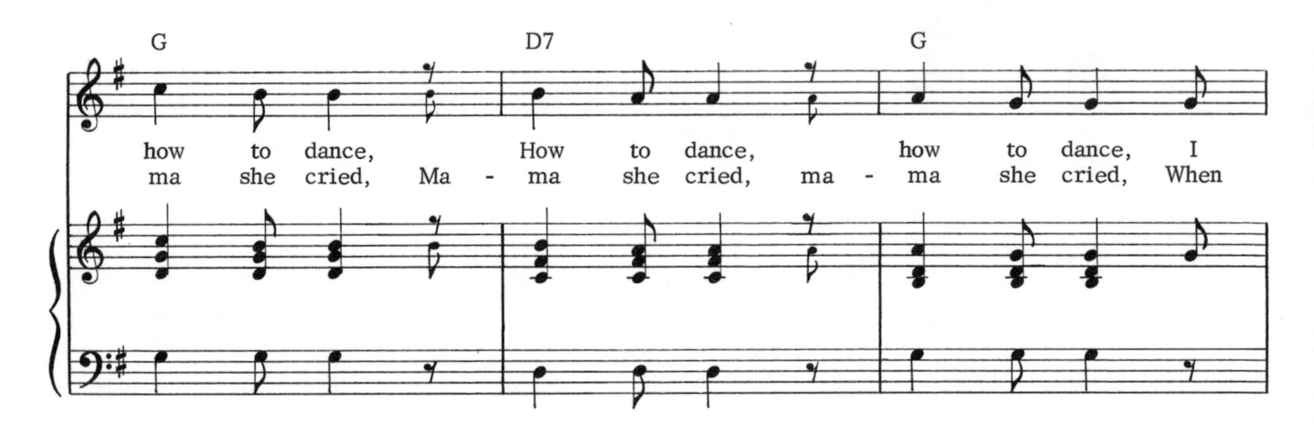
G D7 G
how to dance, How to dance, how to dance, I
ma she cried, Ma - ma she cried, ma - ma she cried, When

C G A7 D
teach the la - dies how to dance, For I'm their pet in the ar - my.
I left home, ma - ma she cried, "He ain't cut out for the ar - my."

Chorus
G C G
I'm Cap - tain Jinks of the Horse Ma - rines, I

3. The first day I went out to drill,
The bugle sound made me quite ill,
At the balance step my hat it fell,
And that wouldn't do for the army.
The officers they all did shout,
They all did shout, they all did shout,
The officers they all did shout,
"Oh, that's the curse of the army."

(Chorus)

4. My tailor's bills came in so fast,
Forced me one day to leave at last,
And ladies too no more did cast
Sheep's eyes at me in the army.
My creditors at me did shout,
At me did shout, at me did shout,
My creditors at me did shout,
"Why, kick him out of the army."

(Chorus)

Old Dan Tucker

Words and Music by Daniel Decatur Emmett 1843

A robust ballad with many stanzas that has become known as a traditional American song. The tune is often used for folk dancing.

Mr. Edwards, the family friend, danced to the fiddle's music like a jumping jack in the moonlight. When it was time to go home, Pa played him down the road with "Old Dan Tucker." LHP, *page 69*

3. I come to town the other night,
   I hear the noise and saw the fight;
   The watchman was arunnin' roun'
   Crying "Old Dan Tucker's come to town."

   (Chorus)

4. Old Dan he went down to the mill
   To get some meal to put in the swill;
   The miller swore by the point of his knife
   He never see'd such a man in his life.

   (Chorus)

5. Tucker is a nice old man,
   He used to ride our darby ram;
   He sent him whizzin' down the hill,
   If he hadn't got up, he'd lay there still.

   (Chorus)

6. Old Dan begun in early life
   To play the banjo and the fife;
   He play the children all to sleep,
   And then into his bunk he creep.

   (Chorus)

Old Grimes

Words adapted from "Old Grimes" by Albert Gorton Greene

Tune: "Auld Lang Syne"   Circa 1873

Pa sang his own version of Greene's song while Ma was making cheese. He thought Old Grimes might have staggered along if his wife hadn't skimmed off every bit of cream. But "She was a mean, tight-fisted woman. Old Grimes got so thin the wind blew him away," Pa said. LHBW, *page 192*

A
D
G
skim - milk cheese, Old Grimes he drank the whey, There

D
A
D
came an east wind from the west And blew Old Grimes a - way.

Polly-Wolly-Doodle

Words and Music Traditional USA

An exuberant bit of foolery, this song is believed to be of Negro or minstrel origin. It has become a favorite of college glee clubs.

When Pa had agreed that he and Laura could buy an organ for Mary, he said: "By jinks! I feel like celebrating. Bring me my fiddle, Half-Pint, and we'll have a little music." HGY, *page 155*

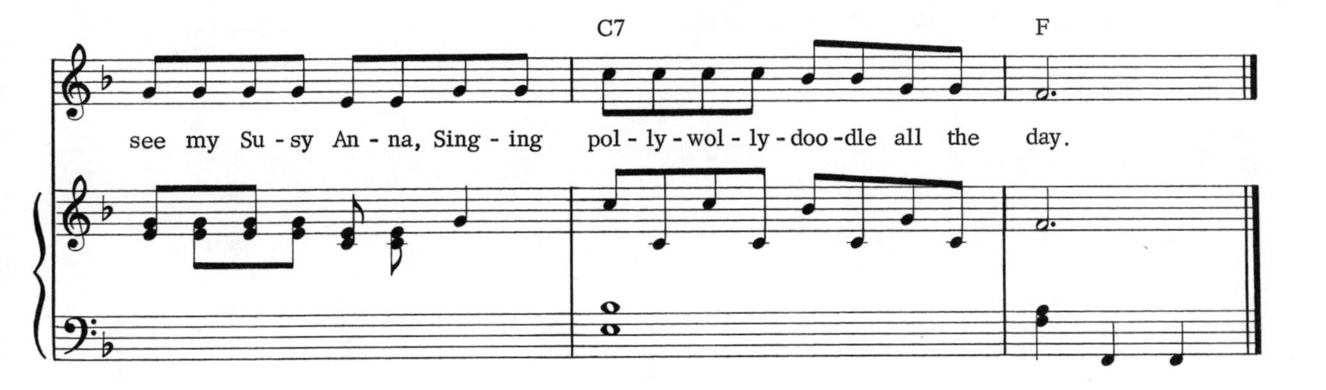

3. Oh, a grasshopper sittin' on a railroad track,
Sing polly-wolly-doodle all the day;
A-pickin' his teeth with a carpet tack,
Sing polly-wolly-doodle all the day.

(Chorus)

4. Oh, I went to bed but it wasn't no use,
Sing polly-wolly-doodle all the day;
My feet stuck out for a chicken roost,
Sing polly-wolly-doodle all the day.

(Chorus)

5. Behind the barn, down on my knees,
Sing polly-wolly-doodle all the day;
I thought I heard that chicken sneeze,
Sing polly-wolly-doodle all the day.

(Chorus)

6. He sneezed so hard with the whoopin' cough,
Sing polly-wolly-doodle all the day;
He sneezed his head and his tail right off,
Sing polly-wolly-doodle all the day.

(Chorus)

Pop! Goes the Weasel

Words and Music Traditional USA

A standard tune at country dances, this song goes back to Old English sources. Once Pa said to Laura and Mary, "Watch, and maybe you can see the weasel pop out this time." "Pop!" said his finger on the string; "Goes the weasel!" sang the fiddle. But Laura and Mary hadn't seen Pa's finger make the string pop. He was so quick they could never catch him. LHBW, *page 99*

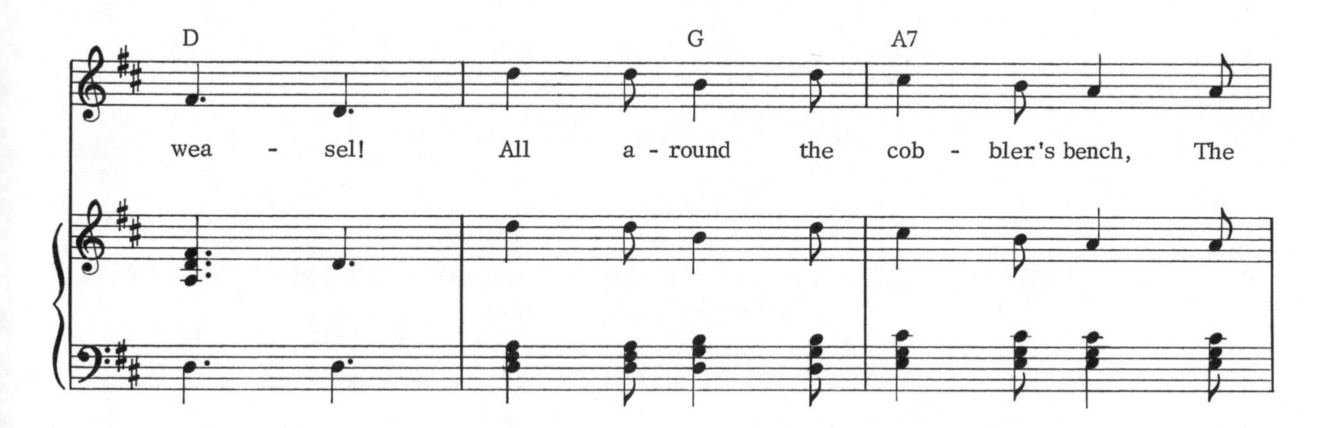
D G A7
wea - sel! All a - round the cob - bler's bench, The

D E7 A G
mon - key chased the wea - sel, The preach - er kissed the

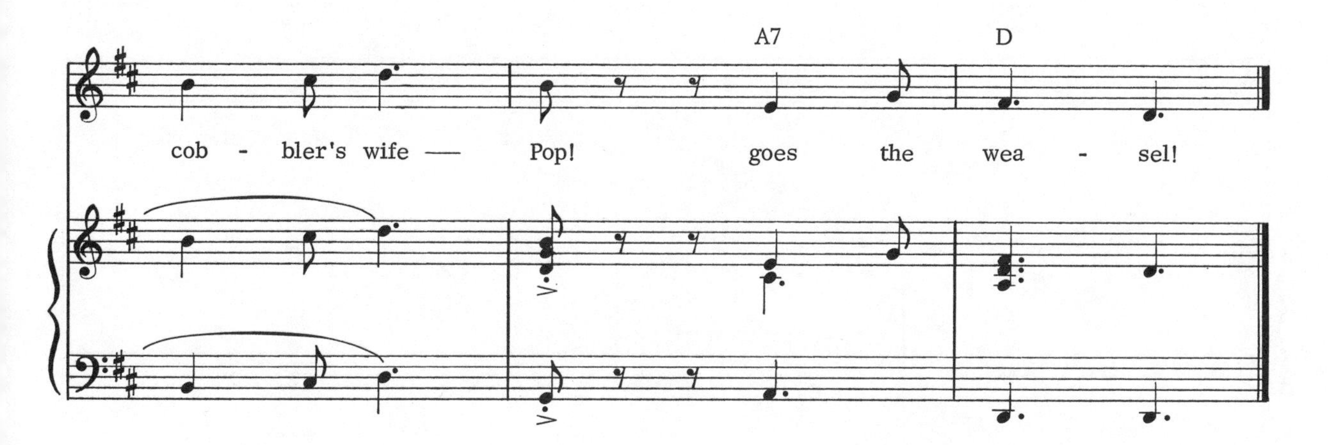
A7 D
cob - bler's wife — Pop! goes the wea - sel!

Uncle John *(A Singing Game)*

Words Traditional USA   Tune: "Yankee Doodle"

This singing game is a love story. It may have been derived from the medieval song in which an imprisoned knight is saved from death by the daughter of a king who keeps him in confinement.

At Laura's first school the little girls always played ring-around-a-rosy at recess till one day she said: "Let's play Uncle John!" BPC, *page 158*

2. "____________" so they say,
Goes acourting night and day,
Sword and pistol by his side,
And "____________" to be his bride.
Takes her by the lily-white hand,
And leads her o'er the water,
Here's a kiss, and there's a kiss,
For Mr. ____________'s daughter.

DIRECTIONS:

1. *The players circle and sing the first verse.*
2. *At the words "governor's daughter" all fall down.*
3. *The last one down stands apart and whispers to a friend the name of a favorite person and then returns to the ring and stands in the center.*
4. *The friend announces the name, and the players circle again, singing the second verse with the names of the couple inserted at the proper places.*
5. *At the end, the ring breaks up. Everyone dances around, clapping his hands.*

Weevily Wheat

Words and Music Traditional USA

There are memories of the Jacobite uprising of 1745 and of Bonnie Prince Charlie in this dance song. It was widely used at play-parties with the steps of the Virginia Reel.

When Pa was safe at home after being snowed in at Plum Creek, he said: "Laura, if you bring me the fiddle box, I'll play you a tune." Then he filled the house with this jaunty music. BPC, *page 336*

3. Coffee grows on white-oak trees,
River flows with brandy,
Choose you one to roam with you
Sweet as 'lasses candy.

(Chorus)

DENTAL
HARDWARE
MERRILL
BOOKS
LIVERY

Patriotic Songs

The Star-Spangled Banner

Words by Francis Scott Key   Music by John Stafford Smith   1814

The words of our national anthem were written during the bombardment of Fort McHenry, near Baltimore, during the War of 1812. They were set to "Anacreon in Heaven," an English melody.

At the Fourth of July celebration when Almanzo was a little boy, the band played and everybody sang: "Oh, say, can you see. . . ." FB, *page 178*

A E
gal - lant - ly stream - ing. And the rock - et's red glare, the bombs burst - ing in
ceals, half dis - clos - es; Now it catch - es the gleam of the morn - ing's first
served us a na - tion! Then con - quer we must, when our cause it is
E7 A E A F#m B7 E
air, Gave proof through the night that our flag was still there.
beam, In full glo - ry re - flect - ed now shines on the stream.
just, And this be our mot - to: "In God is our trust!"
Chorus
E7 A (Bm7 A) D F#7 Bm
Oh! say, does that star - span - gled ban - ner yet
'Tis the star - span - gled ban - ner! Oh, long may it
And the star - span - gled ban - ner in tri - umph shall
A E A E7 A
wave O'er the land of the free and the home of the brave?
wave O'er the land of the free and the home of the brave!
wave O'er the land of the free and the home of the brave!

When Johnny Comes Marching Home

Words and Music by Patrick Gilmore (pseud. Louis Lambert) 1863

Patrick Gilmore, a famous bandmaster, published this song under the pseudonym Louis Lambert. It has been a favorite ever since the Civil War.

The night of Pa's return from working as a harvester, he looked round at Ma and the girls and said: "I have missed this." Then he began to play songs of home. BPC, *page 244*

C E7 Am C
rah, hur - rah; The men will cheer, the
rah, hur - rah; The vil - lage lads and
rah, hur - rah; The lau - rel wreath is
G G7 Am E7
boys will shout, The la - dies they will all turn out, And we'll
lass - ies gay, With ros - es they will strew the way, And we'll
read - y now, To place up - on his loy - al brow, And we'll
Am Dm Am E7 Am E7 Am
all feel gay When John - ny comes march - ing home.
all feel gay When John - ny comes march - ing home.
all feel gay When John - ny comes march - ing home.

Hail Columbia

Words by Joseph Hopkinson   Music by Philip Phile   1798

This song was written at a time when war with France was thought to be inevitable. For many years it rivaled "The Star-Spangled Banner" as one of our great patriotic songs.

After supper the Ingalls family all gathered near the warmth of the stove, and Pa sang: "Hail, ye heroes, Heaven born band!" SSL, *page 154*

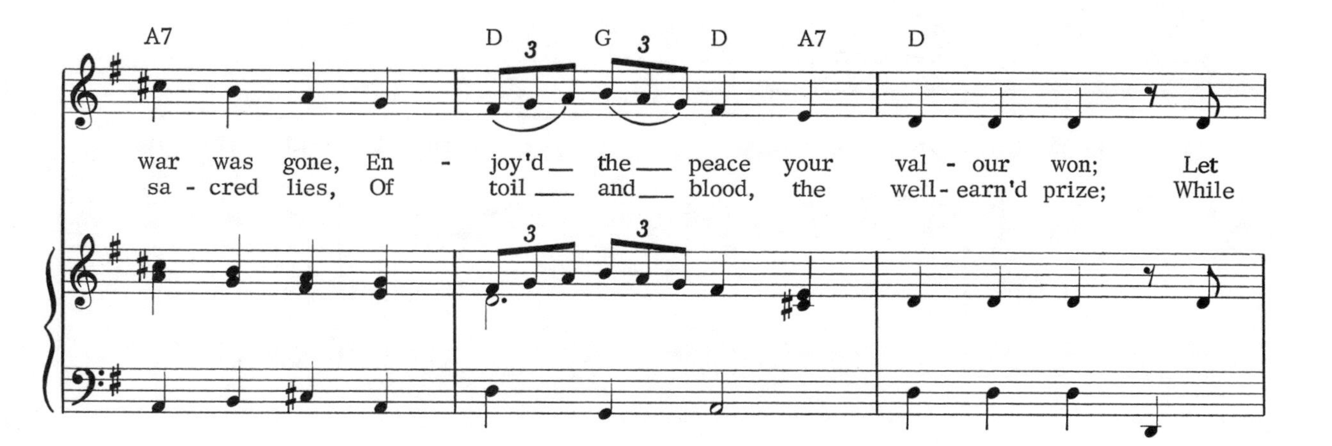
A7 D G D A7 D
3 3
war was gone, En - joy'd the peace your val - our won; Let
sa - cred lies, Of toil and blood, the well - earn'd prize; While

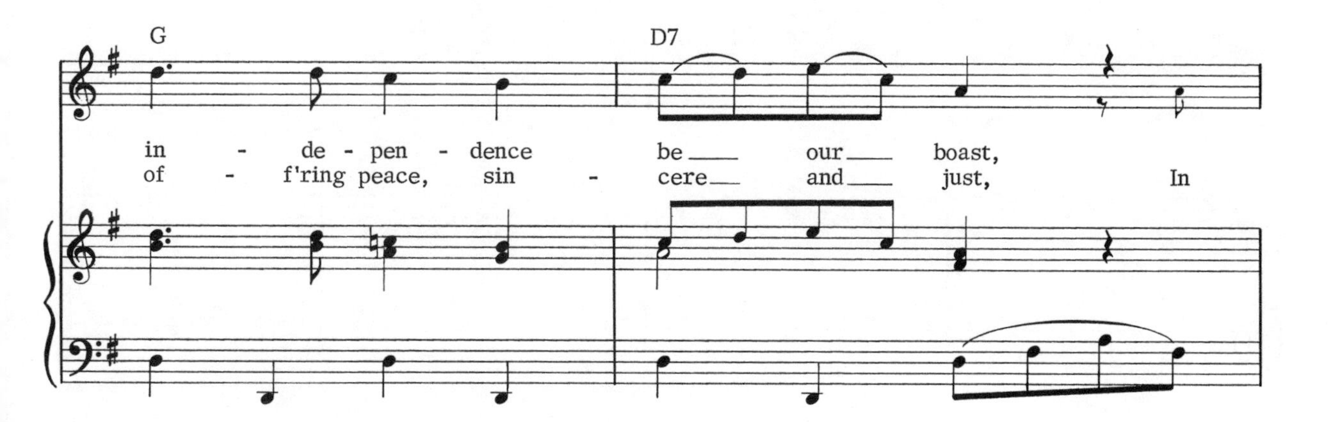
G D7
in - de - pen - dence be our boast,
of - f'ring peace, sin - cere and just, In

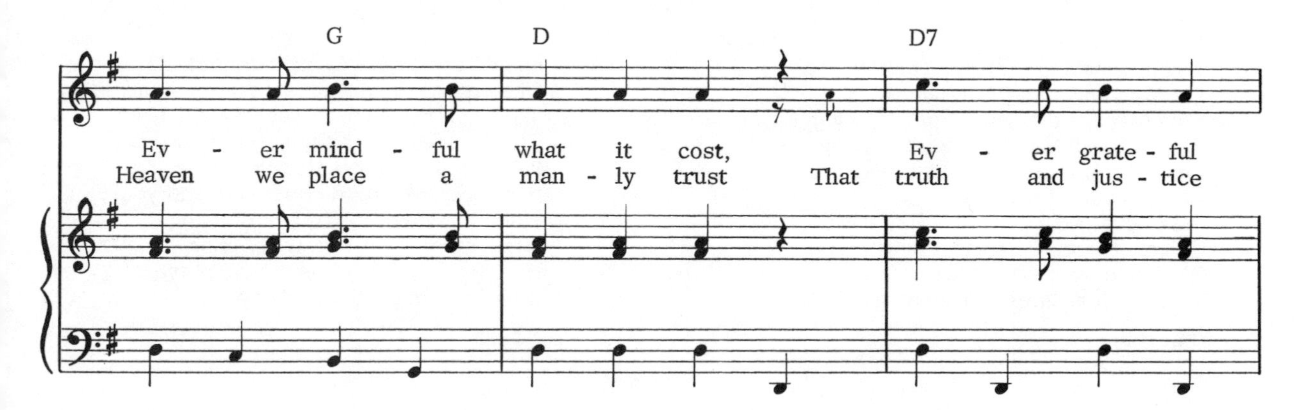
G D D7
Ev - er mind - ful what it cost, Ev - er grate - ful
Heaven we place a man - ly trust That truth and jus - tice

G C D7 G
for the prize, Let its al - tar reach the skies.
will pre - vail, And ev - 'ry scheme of bon - dage fail.

3. Sound, sound the trump of fame!
   Let Washington's great name
   Ring through the world with loud applause!
   Ring through the world with loud applause!
   Let ev'ry clime to freedom dear,
   Listen with a joyful ear!
   With equal skill, with godlike power,
   He governs in the fearful hour
   Of horrid war, or guides with ease
   The happier times of honest peace.

   (Chorus)

4. Behold the chief who now commands!
   Once more to serve his country stands!
   The rock on which the storm will beat,
   The rock on which the storm will beat,
   But arm'd in virtue firm and true,
   His hopes are fix'd on Heaven and you;
   When hope was sinking in dismay,
   When glooms obscured Columbia's day;
   His steady mind, from changes free,
   Resolved on death or liberty!

   (Chorus)

Uncle Sam's Farm

Words and Music by Jesse Hutchinson, Jr.
Original music arranged by N. Barker 1850

Concert tours of singing families were a popular form of musical entertainment in the United States from 1840 to 1860. Best-known were the Hutchinsons. Jesse Hutchinson, Jr., wrote a number of their songs.
Pa sang this song often as he drove westward to the Dakota Territory. Even baby Grace joined in though she didn't bother to follow the tune. SSL, *page 62*

G
D7
room for all cre - a - tion And our ban - ner is un-furl'd, Here's a
great At - lan - tic O - cean Where the sun be - gins to dawn, Leap a -
G
D7
G
gen - 'ral in - vi - ta - tion To the peo - ple of the world.
cross the Rock - y Moun - tains Far a - way to O - re - gon.
Chorus
G
Oh, come a - way! Come a - way!
D
G
C
A7
D
Come a-way, I say! Oh, come a-way! Come a-way! Come right a-way! Oh,

3. While the South shall raise the cotton
   And the West the corn and pork,
   New England manufactories
   Shall do up the finer work,
   For the deep and flowing waterfalls
   That course along our hills,
   Are just the thing for washing sheep
   And driving cotton mills.

   (Chorus)

4. Our fathers gave us Liberty
   But little did they dream,
   The grand results that pour along
   This mighty age of steam,
   For our mountains, lakes, and rivers
   Are all a blaze of fire,
   And we send our news by lightning
   On the telegraphic wire.

   (Chorus)

5. Yes! we're bound to beat the nations
   For our motto's "Go ahead,"
   And we'll tell the foreign countries
   That our people are well-fed,
   For the nations must remember
   That Uncle Sam is not a fool,
   For the people do the voting
   And the children go to school.

   (Chorus)

America

Words by Reverend Samuel Francis Smith   Traditional English Tune   1831

The words to this song were written at the request of Lowell Mason, the "father of public-school music in the United States." They were first sung at a children's celebration of Independence Day in Boston. When Laura heard them, her whole mind seemed to be lighted up by their message of freedom under Divine Law. LTP, *page 76*

3. Let music swell the breeze,
   And ring from all the trees
   Sweet freedom's song;
   Let mortal tongues awake;
   Let all that breathe partake;
   Let rocks their silence break
   The sound prolong.

4. Our father's God to Thee,
   Author of liberty,
   To Thee we sing;
   Long may our land be bright
   With freedom's holy light;
   Protect us by Thy might,
   Great God, our King!

Love and Courtship

The Blue Juniata

Words and Music by Mrs. Marion Dix Sullivan 1844

Although the Juniata is a little river in Pennsylvania, Ma sang this highly romanticized ballad out on the prairie. When Laura asked her where the voice of Alfarata went, Ma answered, "Oh, I suppose she went West. That's what Indians do." Then Pa explained how the government was moving the Indians westward and how the settlers were taking over their land. LHP, *page 235*

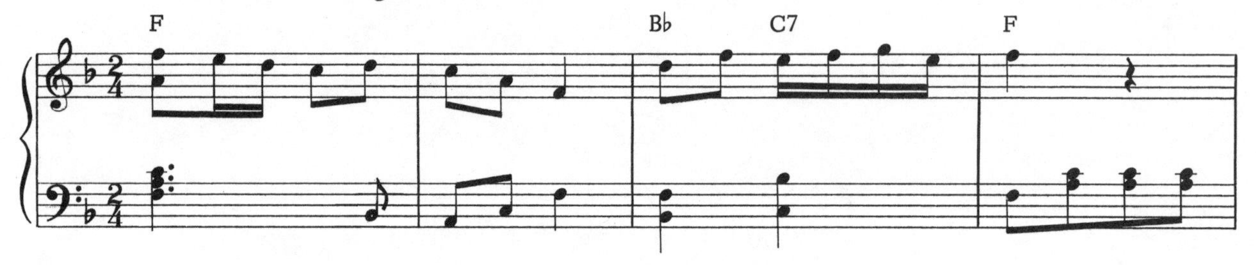

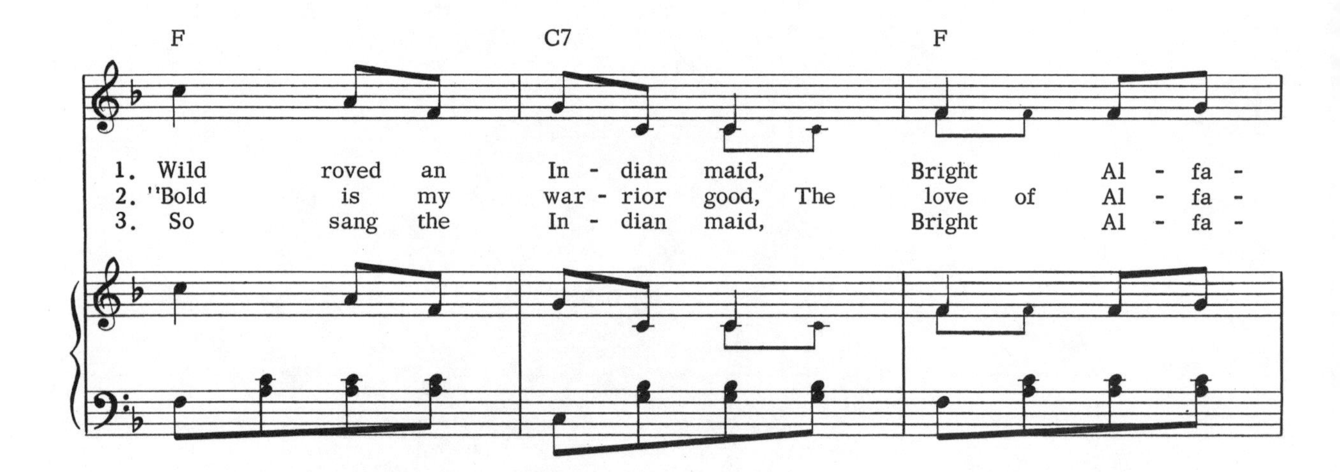

B♭ C7 F
blue — Ju - ni - a - ta. Strong and true my
long the Ju - ni - a - ta. Soft and low he
blue — Ju - ni - a - ta. Fleet - ing years have

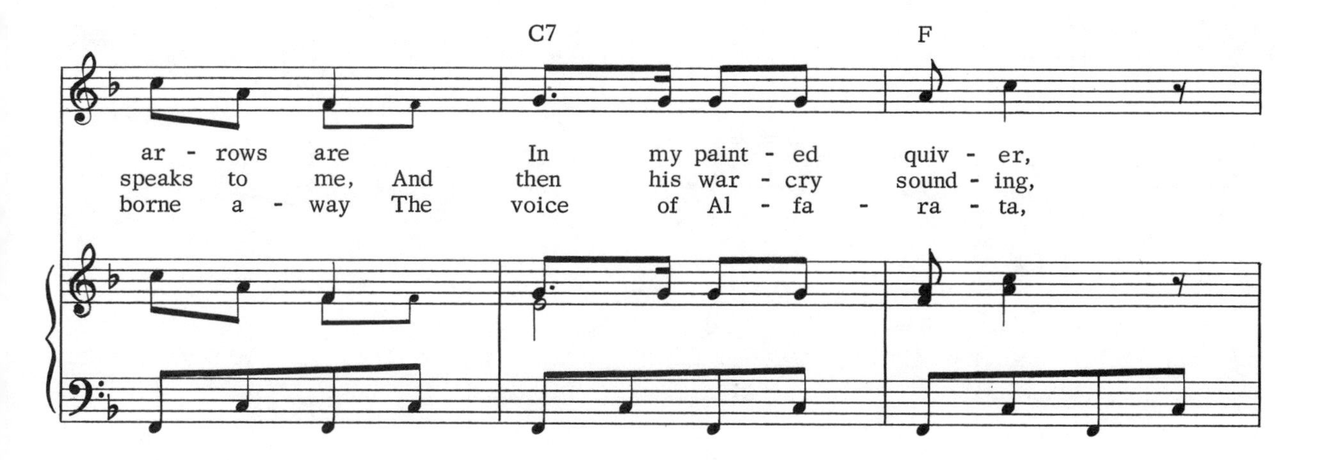
C7 F
ar - rows are In my paint - ed quiv - er,
speaks to me, And then his war - cry sound - ing,
borne a - way The voice of Al - fa - ra - ta,

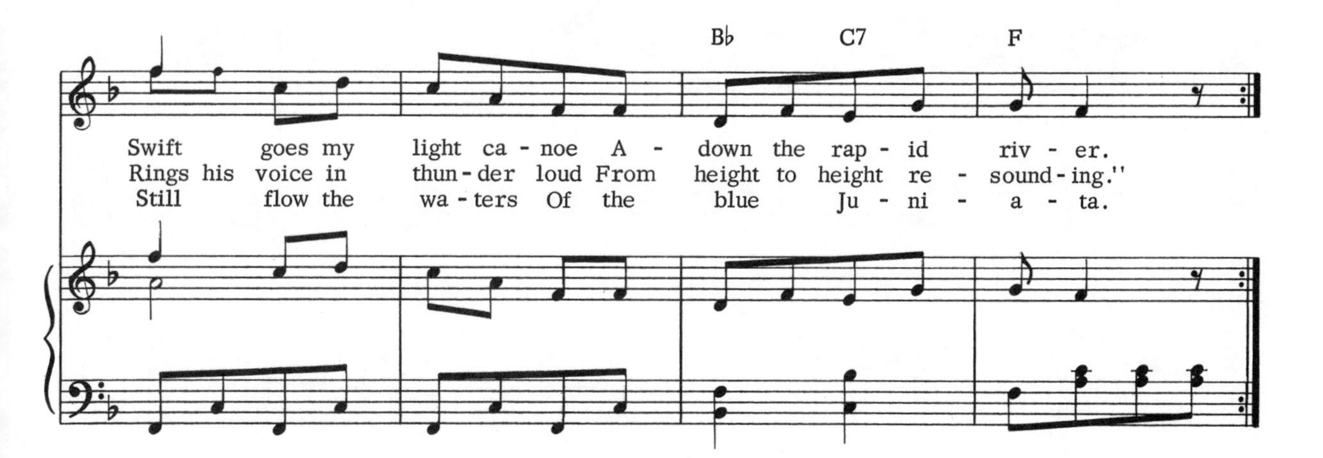
B♭ C7 F
Swift goes my light ca - noe A - down the rap - id riv - er.
Rings his voice in thun - der loud From height to height re - sound - ing."
Still flow the wa - ters Of the blue Ju - ni - a - ta.

F B♭ C7 F

Come In and Shut the Door

Words by J. P. H. Music by J. G. Callcott 1863

One snowy Christmas Eve Laura missed Almanzo, who was visiting his old home far away. He might forget her, she thought, or wish that he had not given her a ring. . . . Someone knocked at the door. When Laura opened it, she could not believe her eyes for there stood Almanzo himself. "Come in!" Pa called. "Come in and shut the door!" HGY, *page 227*

G C G D7 G G7
o - pen, John, As they are pass - ing by! You can - not tell what
whis - pered "No," They meant "Yes" all the while! My fa - ther too will
in the dark, Thought on it in the light; And now my lips shall
C Am E B7 E G7 C G7
they may think, They've said strange things be - fore; And if you wish to
wel - come you, I told you that be - fore; It don't look well to
ut - ter what My heart has said be - fore, Yes, dear - est, I... but
C Dm C G♯dim Am Slower Chorus A7 D
talk a - while, Come in and shut the door.
stand out here, Come in and shut the door. Come in, come
wait a - while, Come in and shut the door.
a tempo
G G7 C F C7 F A♭7 C G7 C
in, come in, come in, come in, come in, Come in and shut the door.

Green Grows the Laurel

Words and Music Traditional USA

A very old song of lovers' parting and reunion. The words "orange and blue" refer to William of Orange. In the United States they were sometimes changed to "red, white, and blue." Out on the prairie Pa sang this to Ma when he was leaving for an overnight trip to town. LHP, *page 207*

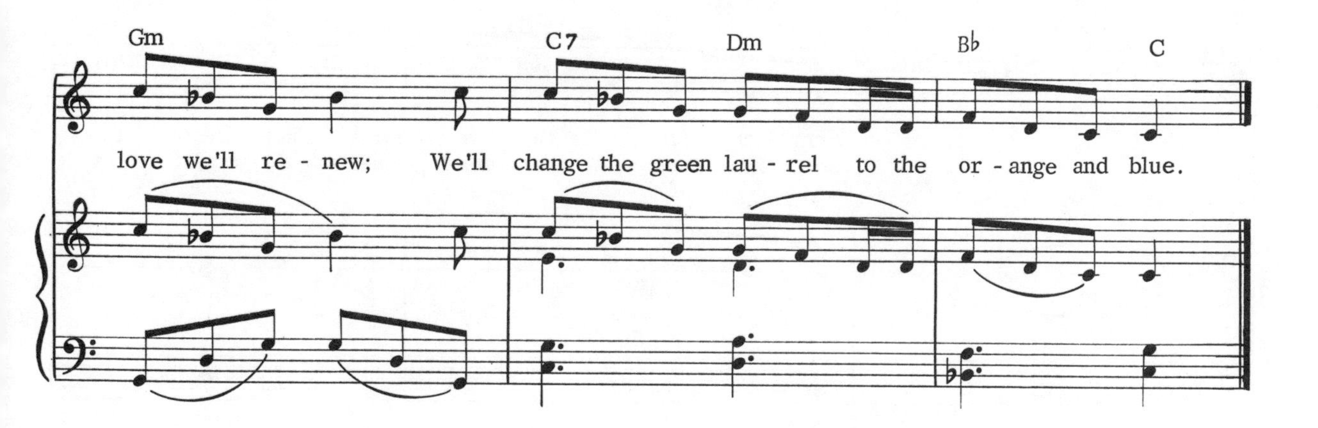

3. She passes my window both early and late,
   And the looks that she gives me, they make my heart break,
   And the looks that she gives me a thousand times o'er,
   "You are the sweetheart I once did adore."

   (Chorus)

4. I ofttimes do wonder why young maids love men,
   I ofttimes do wonder why young men love them;
   But by my experience, I now ought to know
   Young maids are deceivers wherever they go.

   (Chorus)

In Dreamland Far Away

Words by George Birdseye   Music by Hart Pease Danks   1887

George Birdseye was a New York journalist and a friend of Stephen Foster. Hart Pease Danks is the composer of "Silver Threads Among the Gold." Lamplight shone from the windows of the little prairie house. Pa was playing the fiddle; his voice rose with the music of this song, one that he often sang to Ma. HGY, *page 216*

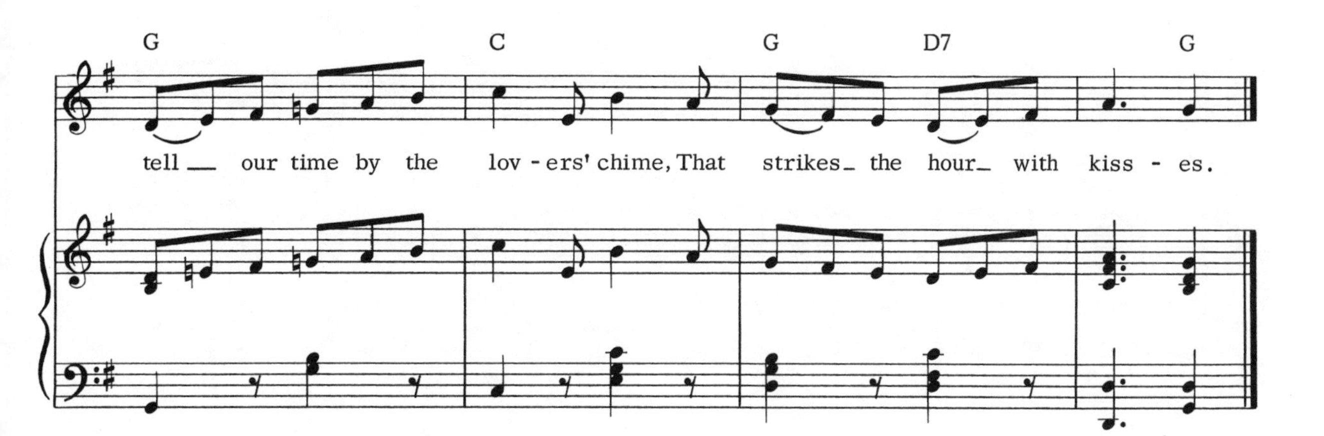

3. Then let us enjoy ev'ry blissful hour!
   Too soon our dreams will break;
   Alas, that we never may have the pow'r
   To live them when we wake!

   (Chorus)

In the Starlight

Words by J. E. Carpenter   Music by Stephen Glover   1843

J. E. Carpenter and Stephen Glover wrote a number of songs together. This charming piece has been included in many collections.

As Almanzo and Laura were driving back from singing school, he said: "I don't know when I ever saw the stars so bright." Softly, Laura began to sing the starlight song. HGY, *page 207*

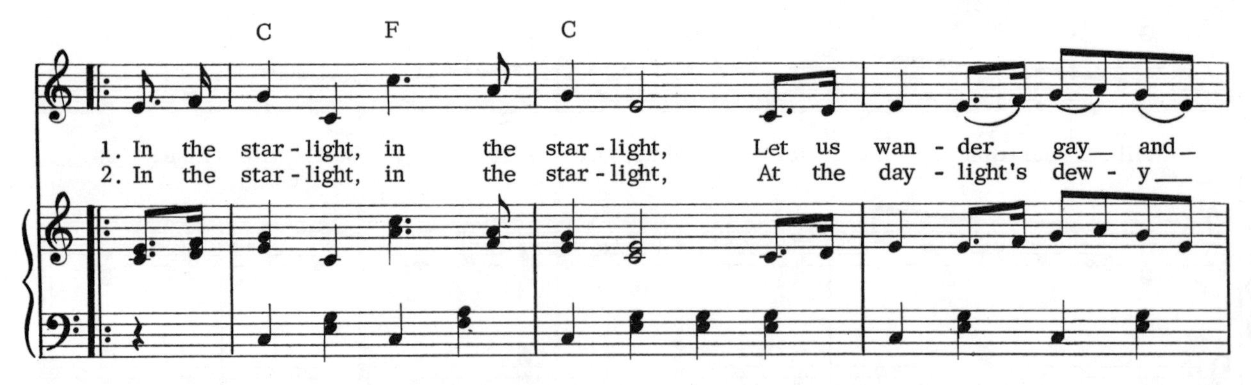

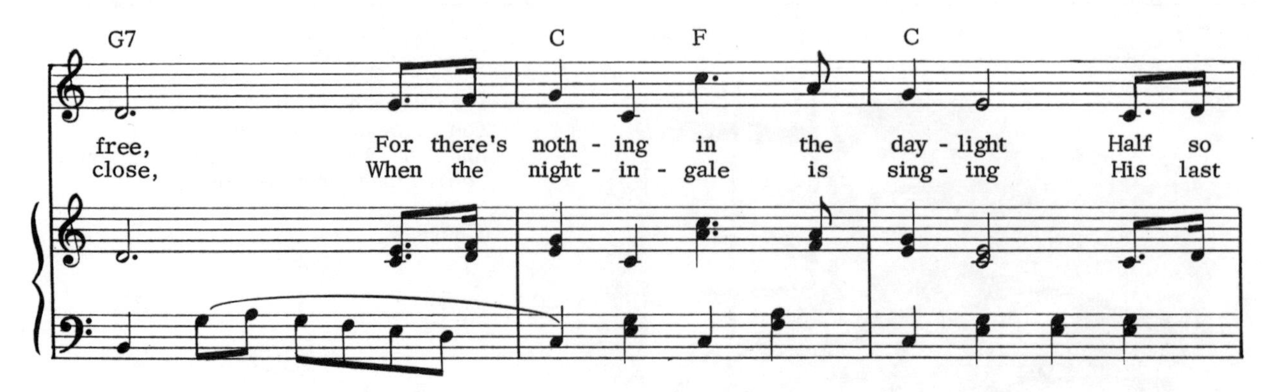

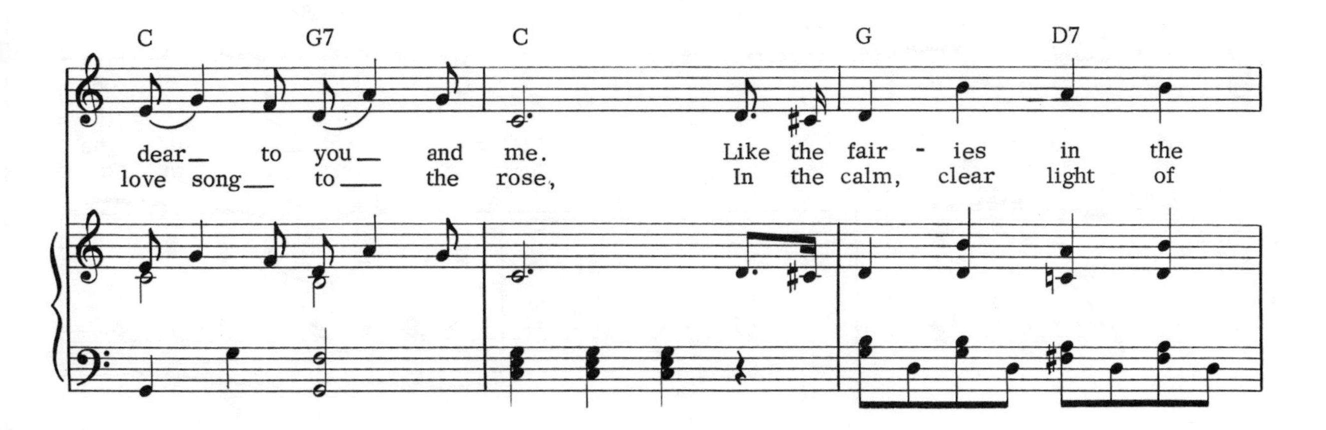
C G7 C G D7
dear to you and me. Like the fair - ies in the
love song to the rose, In the calm, clear light of

G D7 G
shad - ow Of the woods, we'll steal a - long, And our
sum - mer When the breez - es soft - ly play, From the

rit.
D7 G C D7
sweet - est lays we'll war - ble For the night was made for
glit - ter of our dwell - ing We will gen - tly steal a -
rit.

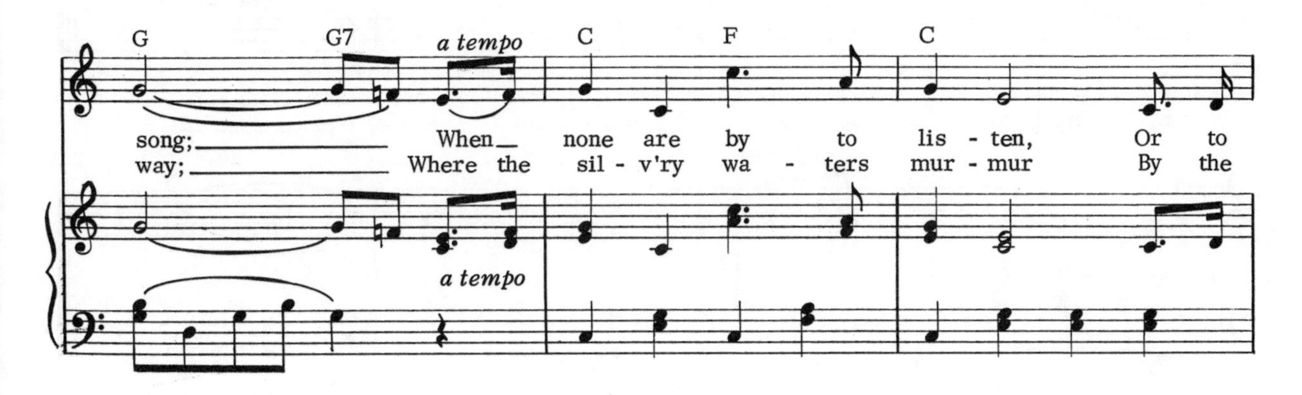
G G7 a tempo C F C
song; When none are by to lis - ten, Or to
way; Where the sil - v'ry wa - ters mur - mur By the
a tempo

C
G7
chide us in our glee, In the star - light, in the
mar - gin of the sea, In the star - light, in the

C
A♭7
C
G7
C
Chorus
G7
star-light, Let us wan-der gay and free. In the star-light, in the
star-light, We will wan-der gay and free. In the star-light, in the
opt. 8va

C
G7
C
star-light, let us wan-der, let us wan-der, In the star - light, in the
star-light, we will wan-der, we will wan-der, In the star - light, in the
opt. 8va

F
C
G7
C
star - light, let us wan - der gay and free.
star - light, we will wan - der gay and free.

Whip-Poor-Will's Song

Words and Music by Harrison Millard 1865

Pa said, "I want to try a song I heard a fellow singing the other day. He whistled the chorus. I believe the fiddle will beat his whistling." Pa sang low and longingly, and "Whip-poor-will" the fiddle answered, fluting and throbbing like the throat of the bird. LTP, *page 136*

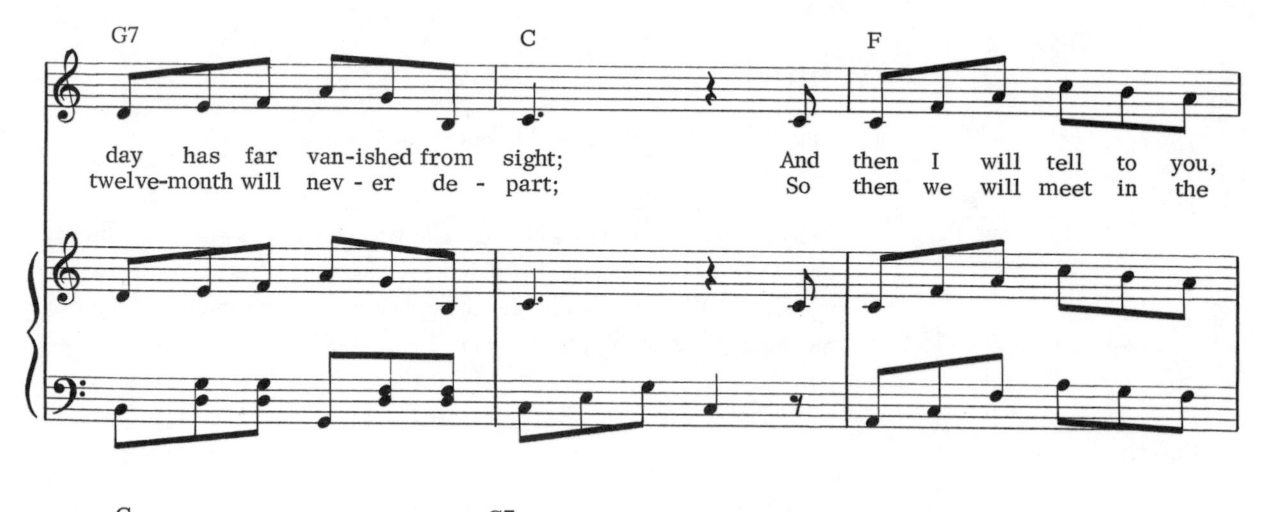
G7
C
F
day has far van-ished from sight;
And then I will tell to you,
twelve-month will nev - er de - part;
So then we will meet in the

C
G7
C
dar - ling, All the love I have cher-ished so long, If
wood -land, Far a - way from the hur - ry - ing throng, And

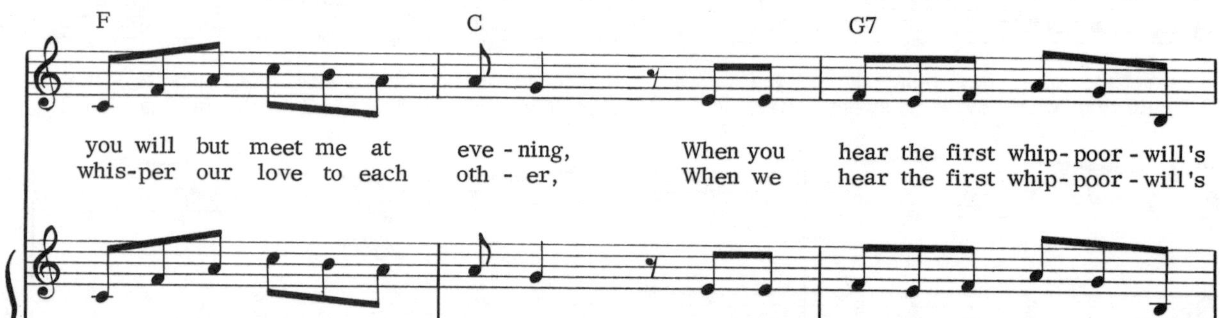
F
C
G7
you will but meet me at eve - ning, When you hear the first whip-poor - will's
whis-per our love to each oth - er, When we hear the first whip-poor - will's

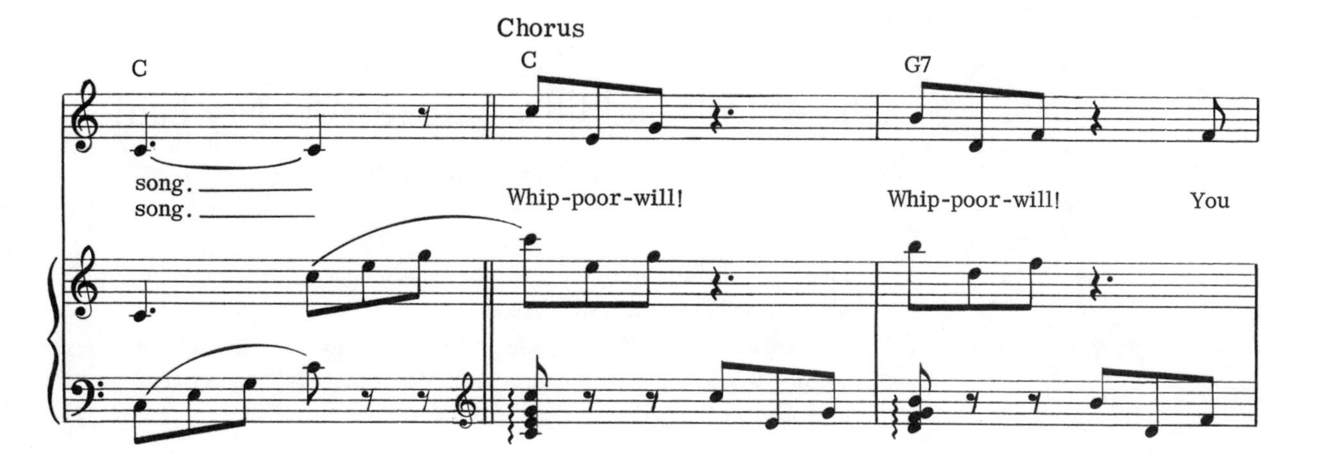

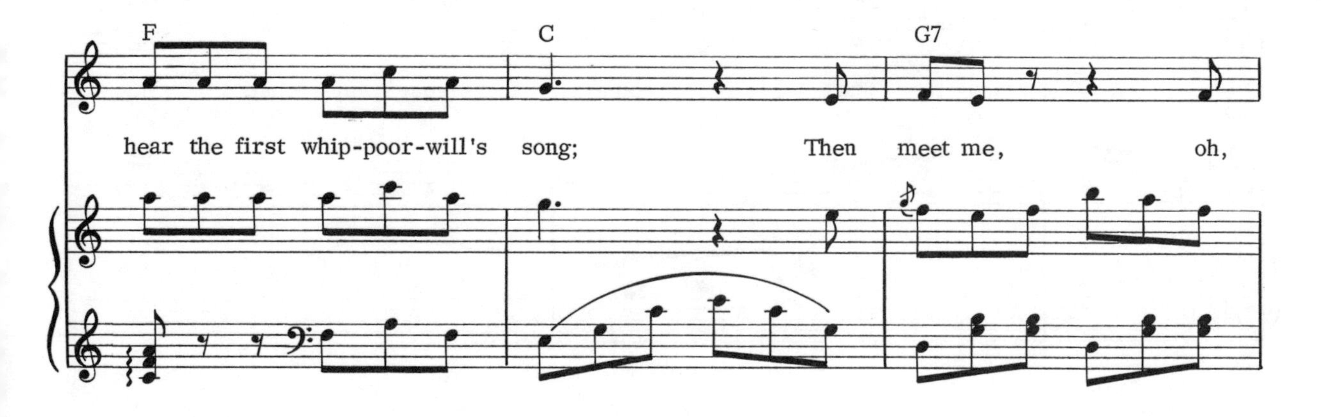

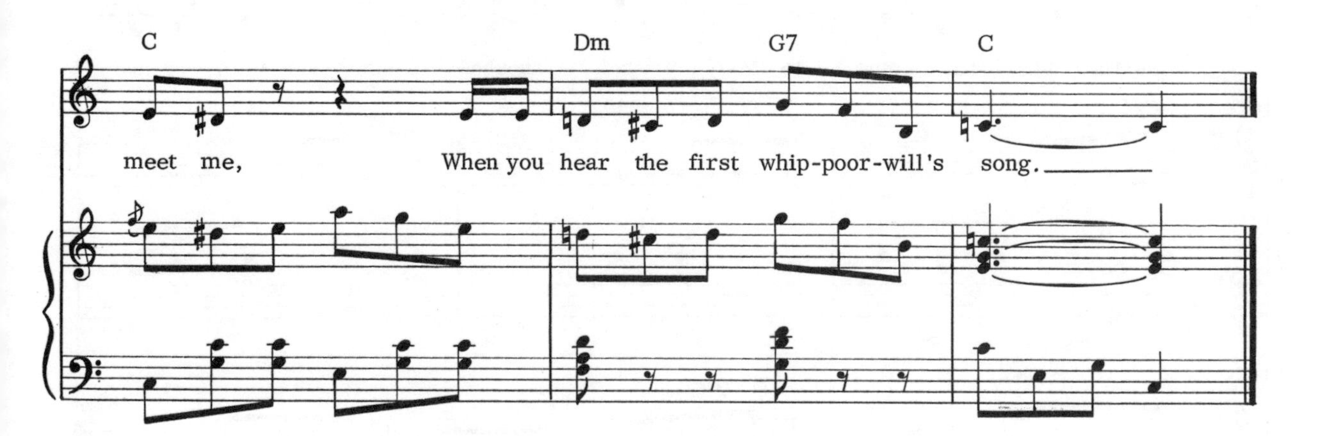

3. And in the long years of the future,
Though our duties may part us awhile,
And on the return of this evening,
We'll be severed by many a mile;
Yet deep in our bosoms we'll cherish
The affection, so fervent and strong,
We pledged to each other this evening,
When we heard the first whip-poor-will's song.

(Chorus)

Oh, Whistle and I'll Come to You, My Lad!

Words by Robert Burns   Traditional Scottish Tune   1799

Like most of Burns' songs, the words of this song are partly traditional, partly his own, and are set to a folk melody.

When Laura sang: "Oh, whistle and I'll come to you, my lad," Almanzo asked: "Would you?" "Of course not!" she answered. "That's only a song."

HGY, *page 184*

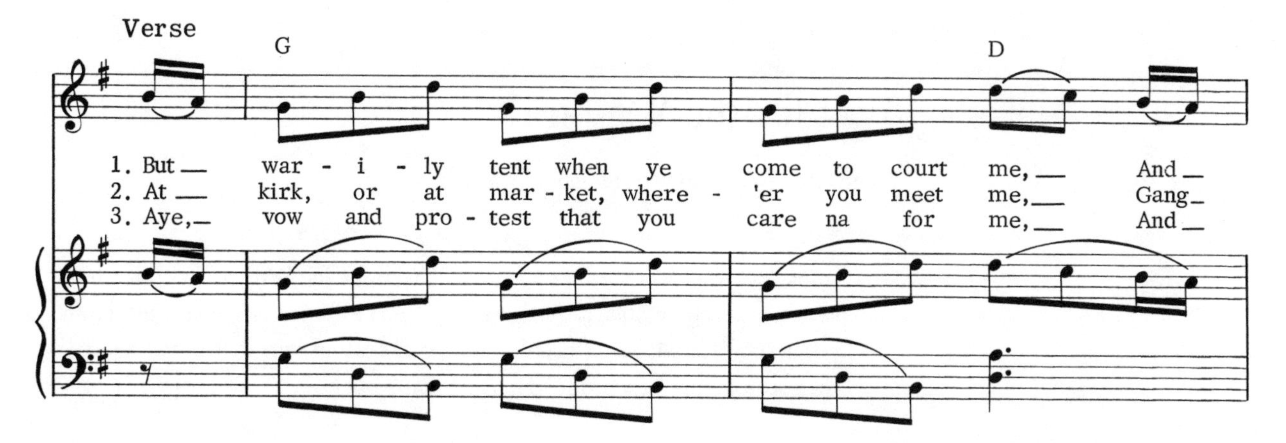
Verse
G
D
1. But__ war - i - ly tent when ye come to court me,__ And__
2. At__ kirk, or at mar - ket, where - 'er you meet me,__ Gang__
3. Aye,__ vow and pro - test that you care na for me,__ And__

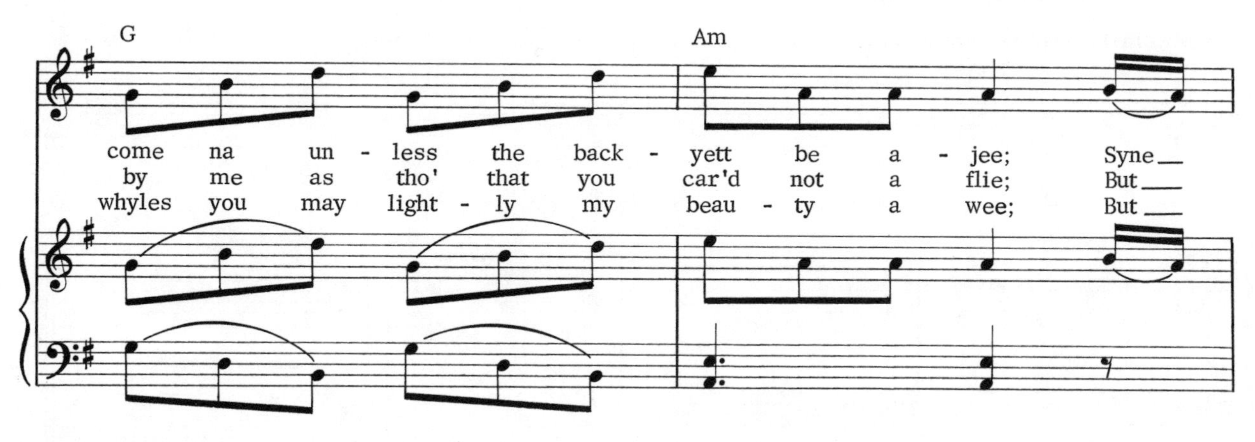
G
Am
come na un - less the back - yett be a - jee; Syne__
by me as tho' that you car'd not a flie; But__
whyles you may light - ly my beau - ty a wee; But__

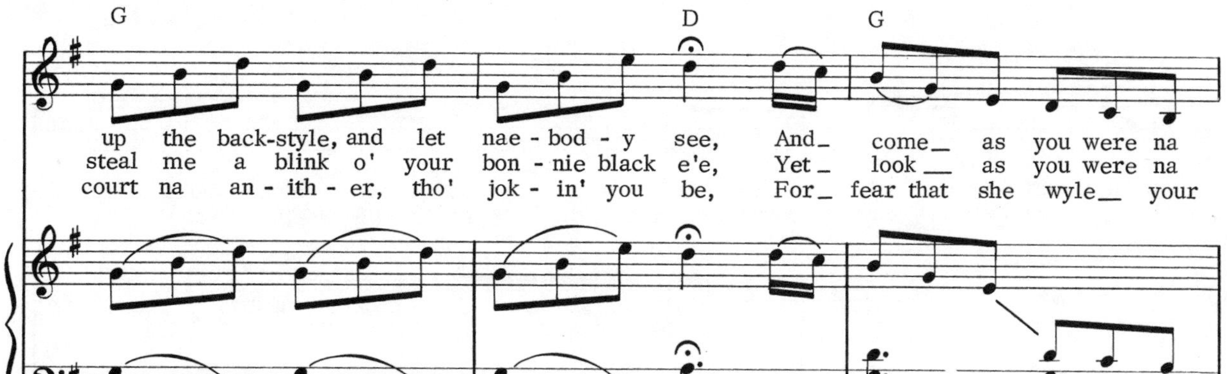
G
D
G
up the back-style, and let nae - bod - y see, And__ come__ as you were na
steal me a blink o' your bon - nie black e'e, Yet__ look__ as you were na
court na an - ith - er, tho' jok - in' you be, For__ fear that she wyle__ your

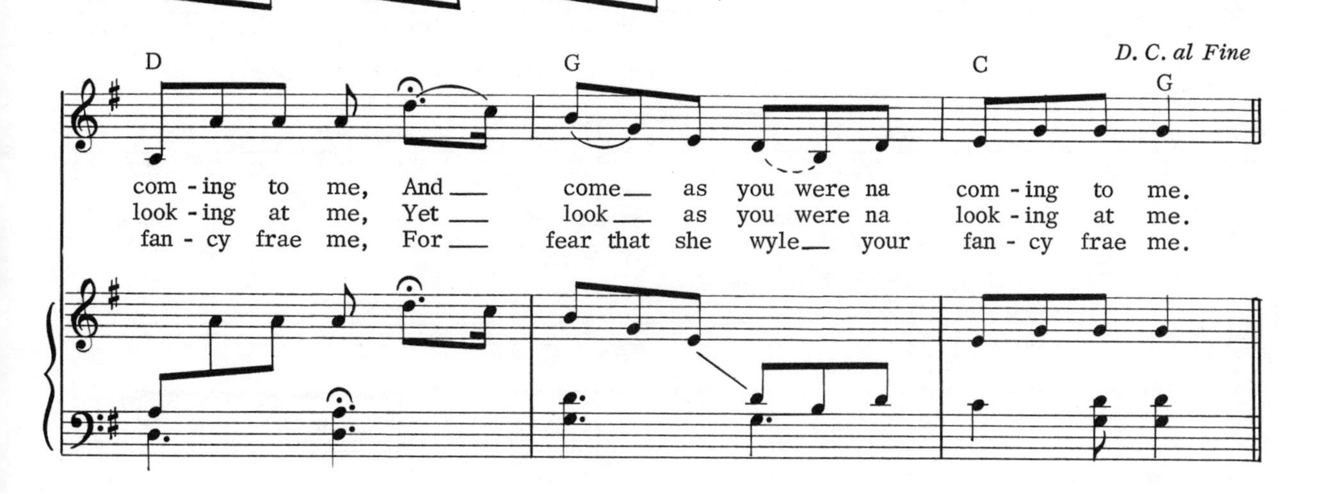
D
G
C
G
D. C. al Fine
com - ing to me, And__ come__ as you were na com - ing to me.
look - ing at me, Yet__ look__ as you were na look - ing at me.
fan - cy frae me, For__ fear that she wyle__ your fan - cy frae me.

Wait for the Wagon

Words and Music Anonymous, USA   Circa 1851

An old favorite that is still heard today, "Wait for the Wagon" has often been paraphrased and used as a campaign song. When Pa began to sing it as the family rode to church, Ma said "Charles" softly to remind him that it was Sunday. Then all together they sang: "There is a happy land. . . ." BPC, *page 181*

3. Your lips are red as poppies,
   Your hair so slick and neat,
   All braided up with dahlias,
   And hollyhocks so sweet.

4. It's ev'ry Sunday morning,
   When I am by your side,
   We'll jump into the wagon,
   And all take a ride.

   (Chorus)

5. Together on life's journey,
   We'll travel till we stop,
   And if we have no trouble,
   We'll reach the happy top.

6. Then come with me, sweet Phillis,
   My dear, my lovely bride,
   We'll jump into the wagon,
   And all take a ride.

   (Chorus)

Beware!

Words by Henry Wadsworth Longfellow   Music by Charles Moulton 1865

The original of Longfellow's poem warns against a flirtatious maiden. But when Cousin Lena sang "Beware!" at Silver Lake, it was about a young man who would prove untrue. As Laura and Lena climbed into the buggy, the black ponies gave a little squeal and ran. Everything went rushing by too fast to be seen. Lena began to sing, and Laura joined in with all her voice. SSL, *page 48*

3. And she has hair of golden hue,
   Take care! take care!
   And what she says, it is not true,
   Beware! beware!

   (Chorus)

4. She gives thee a garland woven fair,
   Take care! take care!
   It is a fool's cap for thee to wear,
   Beware! beware!

   (Chorus)

The Girl I Left Behind Me

Words Traditional USA   Traditional Irish Tune

This tune was first printed in Dublin in 1810. It is the traditional type of music played by a band when troops are leaving. This Western version is also used for square dancing. Pa sang it to Ma when he came back from his long trip to the wheatfields where he had been working as a harvester. BPC, *page 244*

3. She wrote ahead to the place I said
A letter to remind me;
She says, "I am true; when you get through
Ride back and you will find me."
The sweet little girl, the pretty little girl,
The girl I left behind me,
She says, "I am true; when you get through
Ride back and you will find me."

4. If ever I get off the trail,
And the Indians they don't find me,
I'll make my way straight back again
To the girl I left behind me.
The sweet little girl, the pretty little girl,
The girl I left behind me,
I'll make my way straight back again
To the girl I left behind me!

The Big Sunflower

Words and Music by Bobby Newcomb 1868

The theme song of Billy Emerson, the well-known minstrel, this cheerful tune was Pa's "trouble song." He sang it when blizzards turned the windows into a white blur and snow blew through every crack until it had to be shoveled off the beds in the morning. SSL, *page 250*

D7
G
A7
dark dress trimmed in green. Her eyes are bright as
ask her to be mine. But the an - swer I re -
she had shak - en me. She said she real - ly

D
Am
B7
Em
eve - ning stars, So lov - ing and so shy, And the
ceived next day, How could she treat me so? In -
felt quite sad To cause me such dis - tress; And

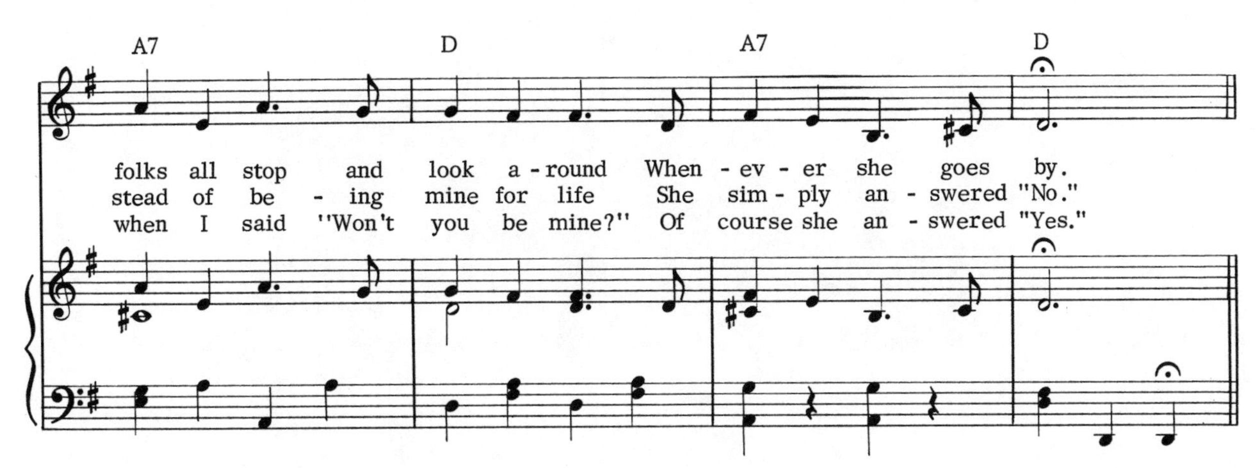
A7
D
A7
D
folks all stop and look a - round When - ev - er she goes by.
stead of be - ing mine for life She sim - ply an - swered "No."
when I said "Won't you be mine?" Of course she an - swered "Yes."

Chorus
D7
G
Oh, I am as hap - py as a big sun - flower That

Am G Em B7 Em
nods and bends in the breez - es, And my heart is as light as the

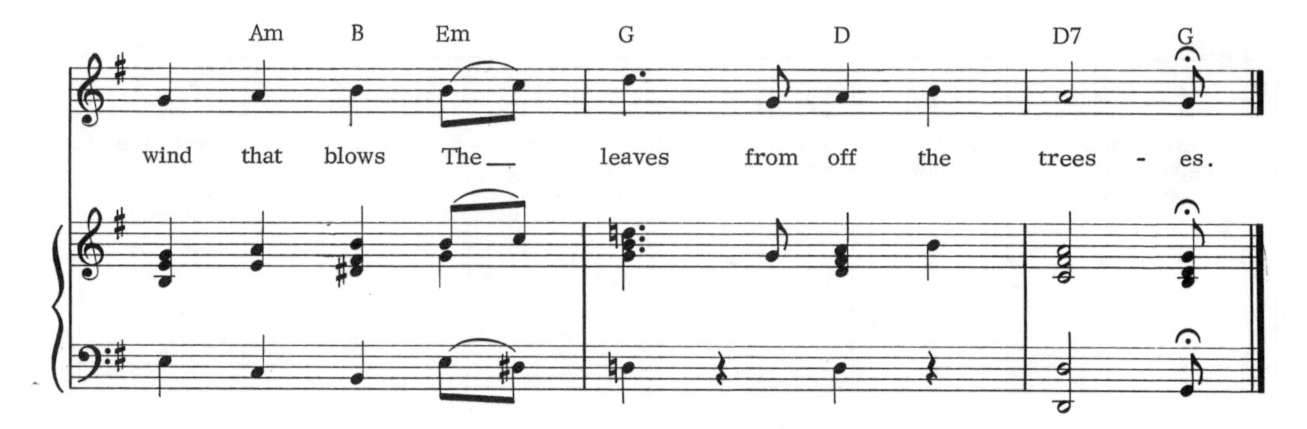
Am B Em G D D7 G
wind that blows The leaves from off the trees - es.

The Gum-Tree Canoe

Words by S. S. Steele   Music by A. F. Winnemore   1847

An old-time minstrel standby, this song is also called "Tombigbee River." When it was time for Laura to go to sleep in the covered wagon, the voice of the fiddle began a long swinging rhythm. As her eyelids closed she seemed to drift over endless seas of prairie grasses to the sound of "Row away, row o'er the waters so blue." LHP, *page 335*

3. With my hands on the banjo and toe on the oar,
   I sing to the sound of the river's soft roar,
   While the stars they look down at my Julia so true
   And dance in her eye in our gum-tree canoe.

   (Chorus)

4. One night the stream bore us so far away
   That we couldn't come back so we thought we'd just stay,
   Oh, we spied a tall ship with a flag of true blue,
   And it took us in tow with our gum-tree canoe.

   (Chorus)

A Railroad Man for Me

Words and Music Traditional USA

A "courting song," many examples of which are found in American folklore. At Silver Lake, Laura and Lena met every morning and every evening to take care of the cows. They led them to drink and moved the picket pins to fresh grass; then they did the milking and sang. Sometimes they sang softly about marrying a railroad man. SSL, *page 93*

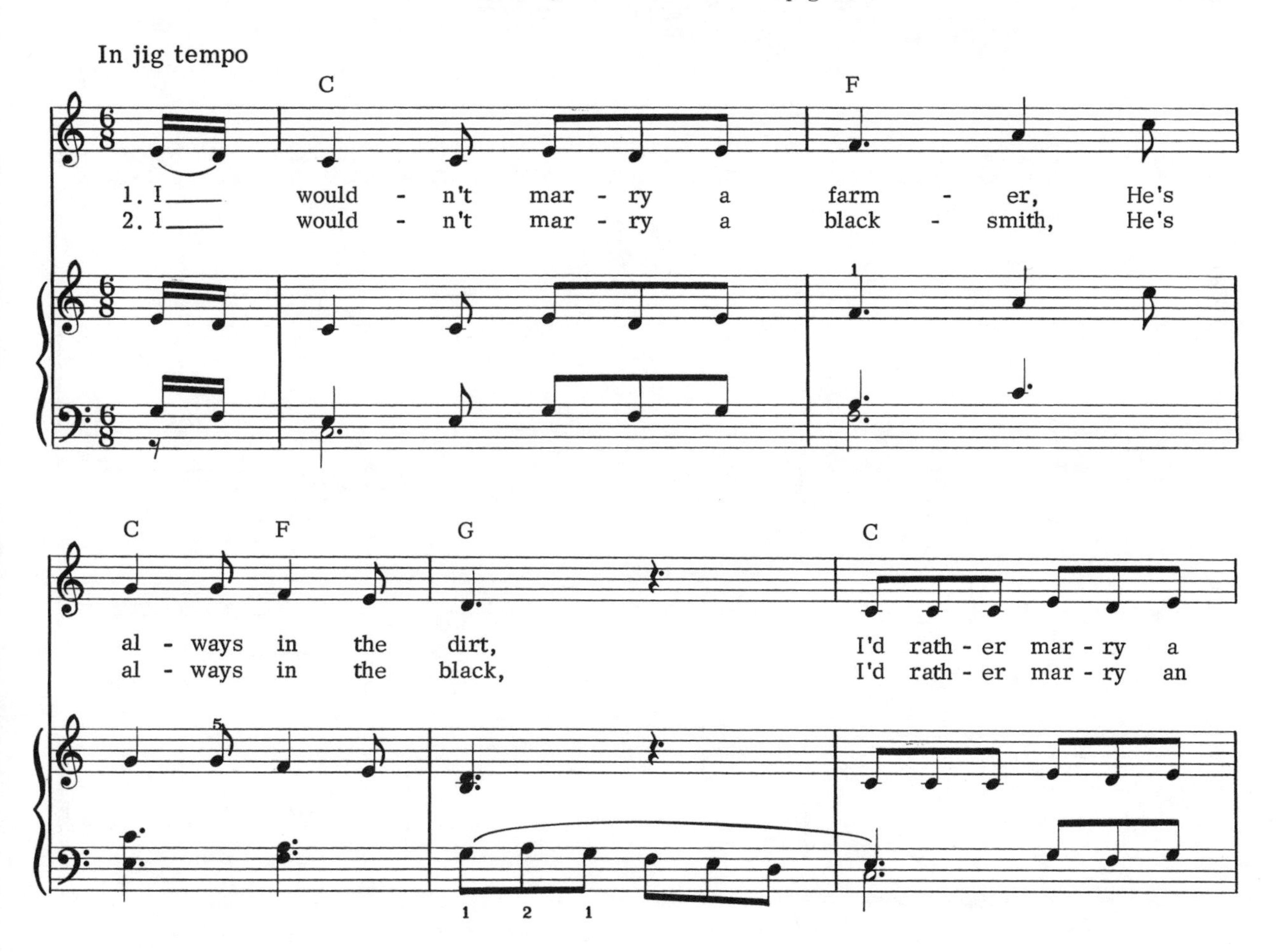

F
G7
C
rail - road man Who wears a strip - ed shirt!
en - gi - neer That throws the throt - tle back.
Chorus
C
F
Oh, a rail - road man, a rail - road man, A
C
G7
C
C7
rail - road man for me! I'm going to mar - ry a
F
C
G7
C
rail - road man, A rail-road-er's bride I'll be!

My Heart Is Sair

Barbary Allen

Words and Music Traditional English

This old ballad was brought to this country by the early colonists. There are many variants of the words and music, but the story remains essentially the same. Moonlight shone through the southern window and touched Pa's face and hands and the fiddle as the bow moved smoothly over the strings while he sang.

SSL, *page 290*

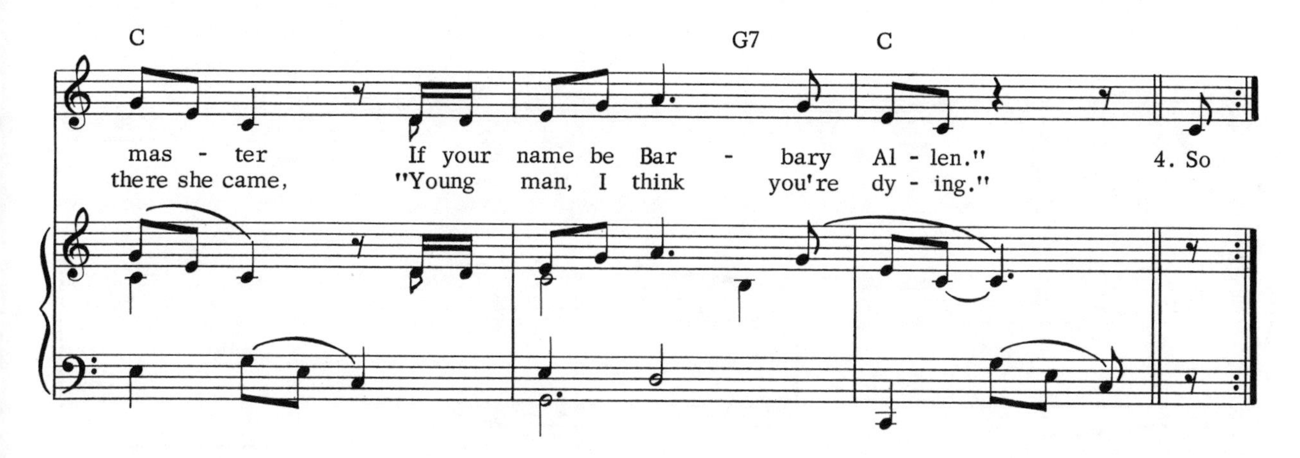

5. He turned his face unto the wall,
And death was with him dealin',
"Adieu, adieu, to all my friends,
Adieu to Barbary Allen."

6. As she was walking o'er the fields,
She heard the bells aknellin',
And every stroke did seem to say
"Unworthy Barbary Allen."

7. When he was dead and laid in grave,
Her heart was struck with sorrow,
"O Mother, Mother, make my bed,
For I shall die tomorrow."

8. She on her deathbed as she lay
Begged to be buried by him,
And sore repented of the day
That she did e'er deny him.

9. "Farewell," she said, "ye virgins all,
And shun the fault I fell in,
Henceforth take warning by the fall
Of cruel Barbary Allen."

Bonny Doon

Words by Robert Burns   Traditional Scottish Tune   1792

In a letter written in 1794, Burns says this tune "was composed a good many years ago by an amateur playing on the black keys of the harpsichord." When everyone sang together in the surveyors' house at Silver Lake, Laura had never been so happy, and she was happiest of all when they were singing this plaintive air. SSL, *page 213*

G
Ye'll break my heart, ye lit - tle birds, That
Wi' light - some heart I pu'd a rose, Full

D G D
wan - ton through the flow - 'ring thorn, Ye mind me of de -
sweet up - on its thorn - y tree; But my false lov - er

G D G C D7 G
part - ed joys, De - part - ed nev - er to re - turn.
stole the rose, And left the thorn be - hind wi' me.

Highland Mary

Words by Robert Burns   Traditional Scottish Tune   1799

Burns wrote to his friend George Thomson about the poem on which this song is based: "It pleases myself; I think it is in my happiest manner." It appeared in Thomson's *Scottish Airs*, set to the tune of "Katherine Ogle." This was Mary's favorite song. "It's sweet," she said. "It's sweet but it's sad," said Laura. SSL, *page 154*

3. Wi' mony a vow and lock'd embrace,
Our parting was fu' tender,
And, pledging aft to meet again,
We tore oursels asunder;
But, oh, fell death's untimely frost,
That nipped my flower sae early!
Now green's the sod and cauld's the clay
That wraps my Highland Mary!

4. Oh, pale, pale now those rosy lips
I oft ha'e kiss'd sae fondly!
And closed for aye the sparkling glance,
That dwelt on me sae kindly!
And mouldering now in silent dust,
That heart that lo'ed me dearly;
But still within my bosom's core
Shall live my Highland Mary.

Lily Dale

Words and Music by H. S. Thompson 1852

This song is a favorite lament for a departed maiden. The melody became the theme for a schottische with variations, as well as for an ornate piano version. It was Christmas Eve in the sod house beside Plum Creek. Pa tuned the fiddle, rosined the bow, and sang about sweet Lily Dale. BPC, *page 336*

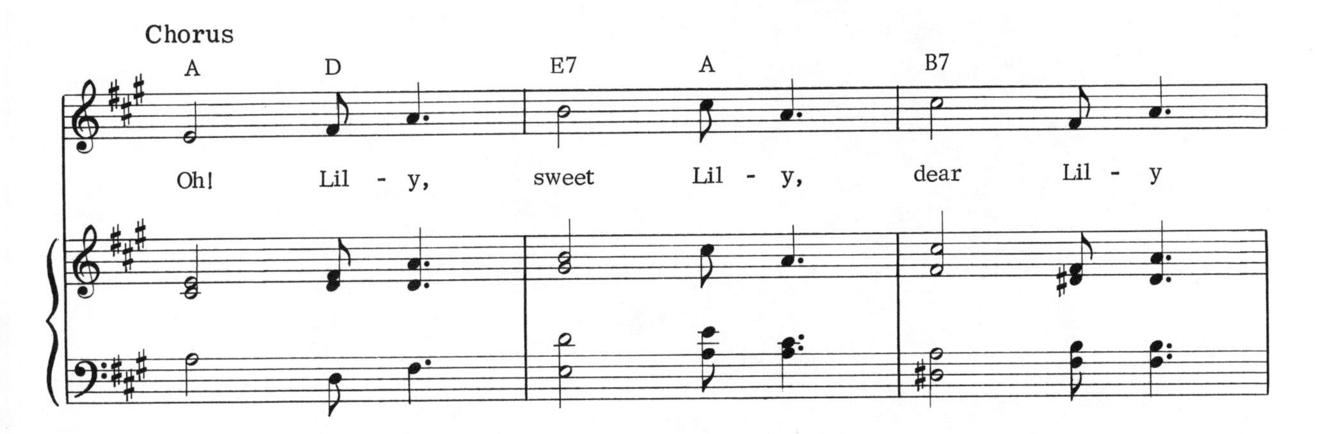

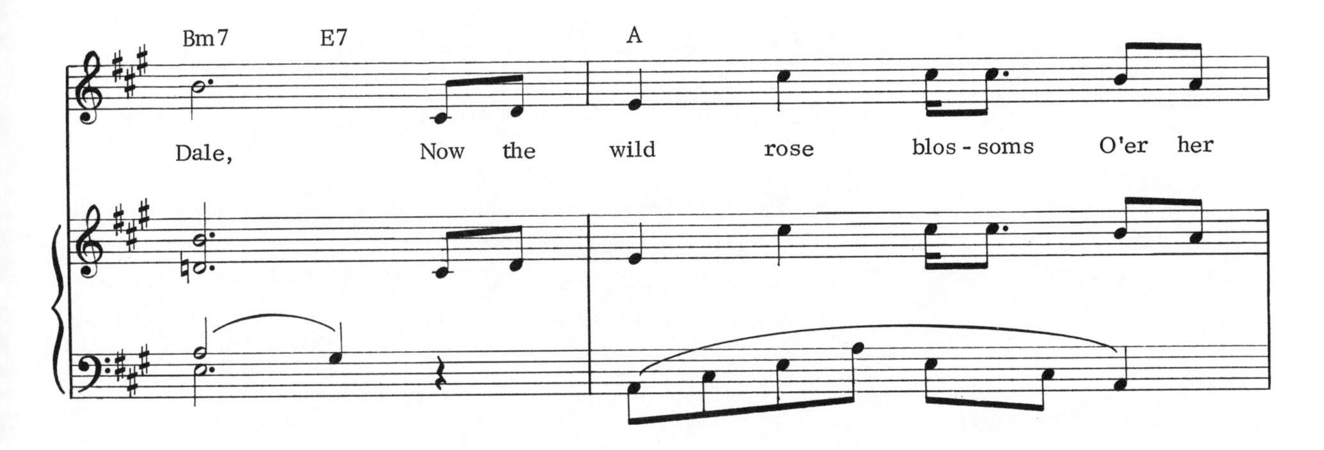

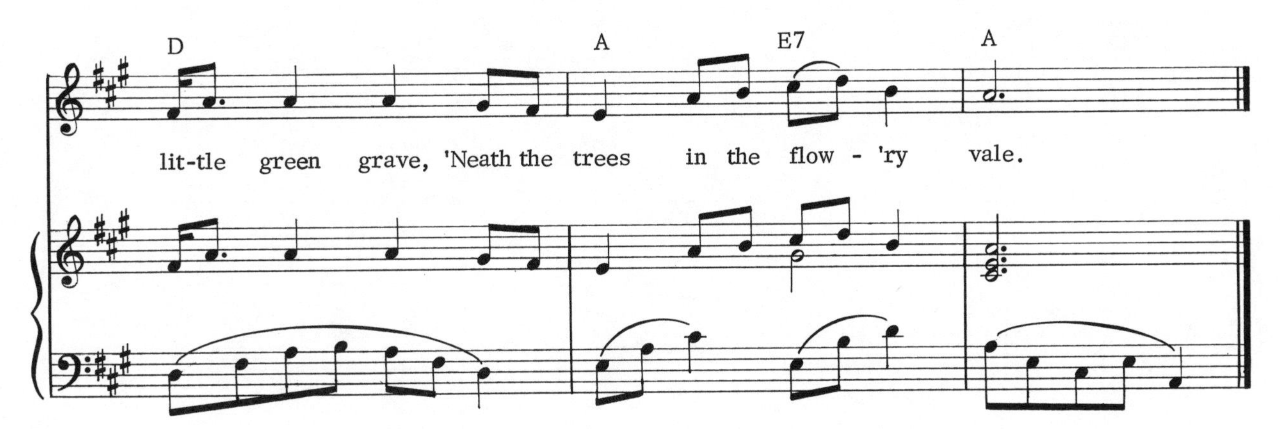

3. "'Neath the chestnut tree,
Where the wild flowers grow,
And the stream ripples forth through the vale,
Where the birds shall warble
Their songs in the spring
There lay poor Lily Dale."

(Chorus)

My Heart Is Sair for Somebody

Words by Robert Burns   Traditional Scottish Tune   1796

There may be echoes of Jacobite sentiment in this song, for James Stuart, the Old Pretender, was spoken of as "Somebody."

The house on the prairie was full of Christmas plans and secrets; there were popcorn balls and little bags of candy in pink mosquito netting. Then Pa said, "Let's have a little music before we begin on these good things." HGY, *page 226*

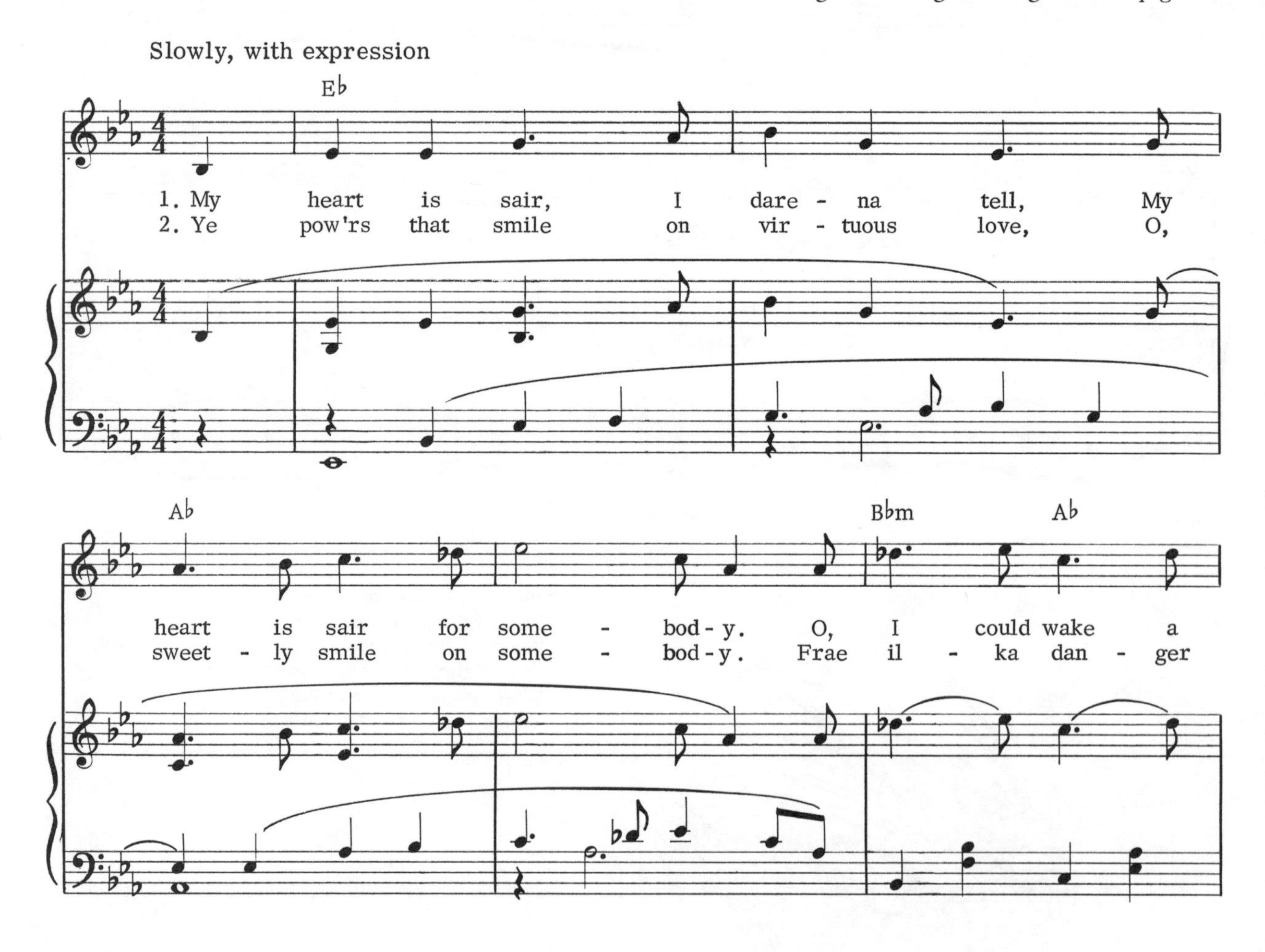

Bbm Eb Ab Cm7 Fm Cm
win - ter night, A' for the sake o' some - bod - y!
keep him free, And send me safe my some - bod - y.
Chorus
Eb
O - hone! for some - bod - y!
Ab Bbm Ab
O - hey! for some - bod - y! I could range the
I would do, what
Bbm Eb Ab Cm7 Fm Cm
world a - round For the sake o' some - bod - y.
would I not, For the sake o' some - bod - y?

Kitty Wells

Words by Thomas Sloan, Jr.   Music by Charles E. Atherton   Circa 1850

Often called "Katy Wells," this song was handed down from memory in numerous versions. It was widely sung in rural areas of the United States.

Laura and Mary were tucked in the trundle bed. Ma's hands were busy sewing by the lamplight. Pa was greasing his boots. He whistled cheerfully as he worked, and then he sang this ballad. LHBW, *page 116*

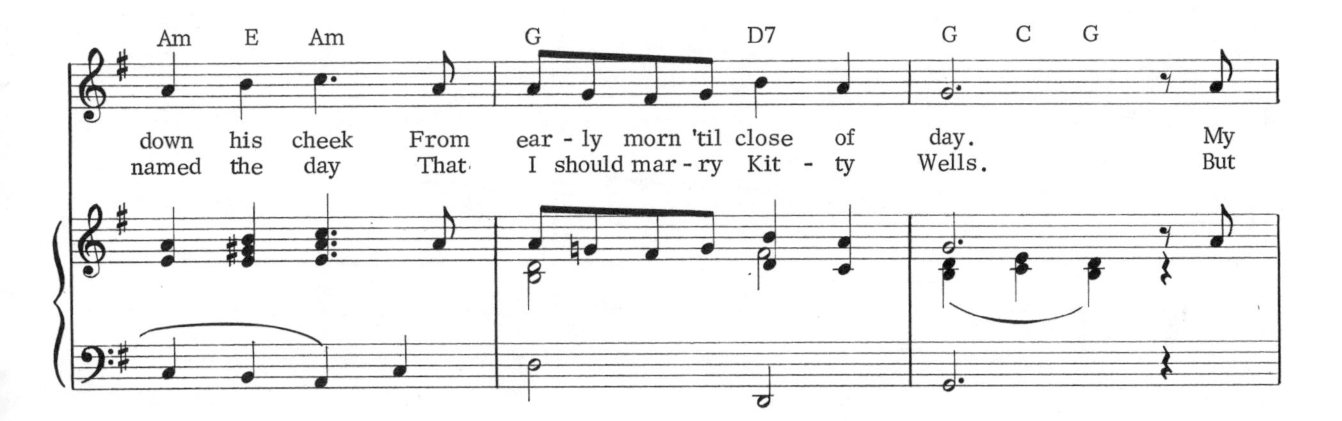
Am E Am G D7 G C G
down his cheek From ear - ly morn 'til close of day. My
named the day That I should mar - ry Kit - ty Wells. But

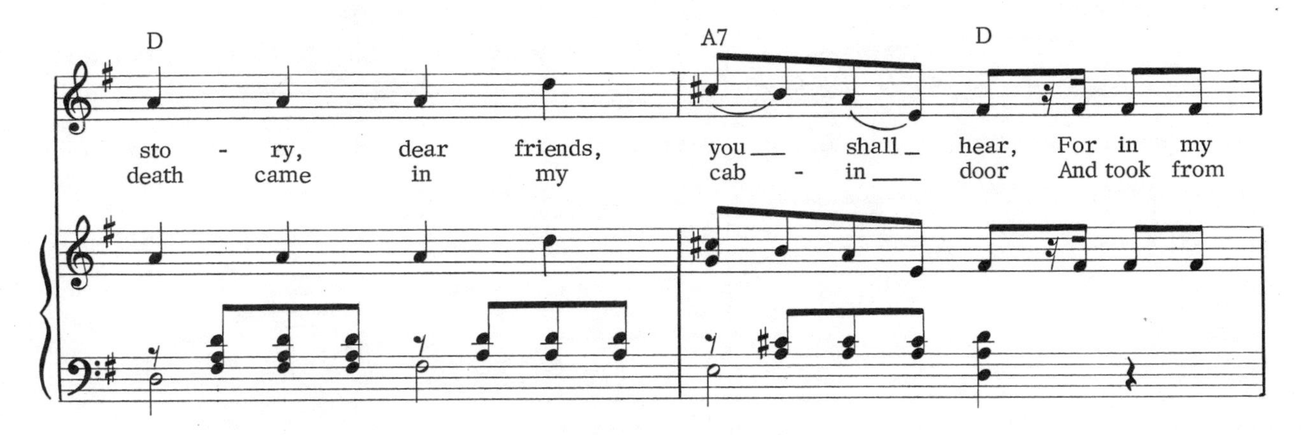
D A7 D
sto - ry, dear friends, you shall hear, For in my
death came in my cab - in door And took from

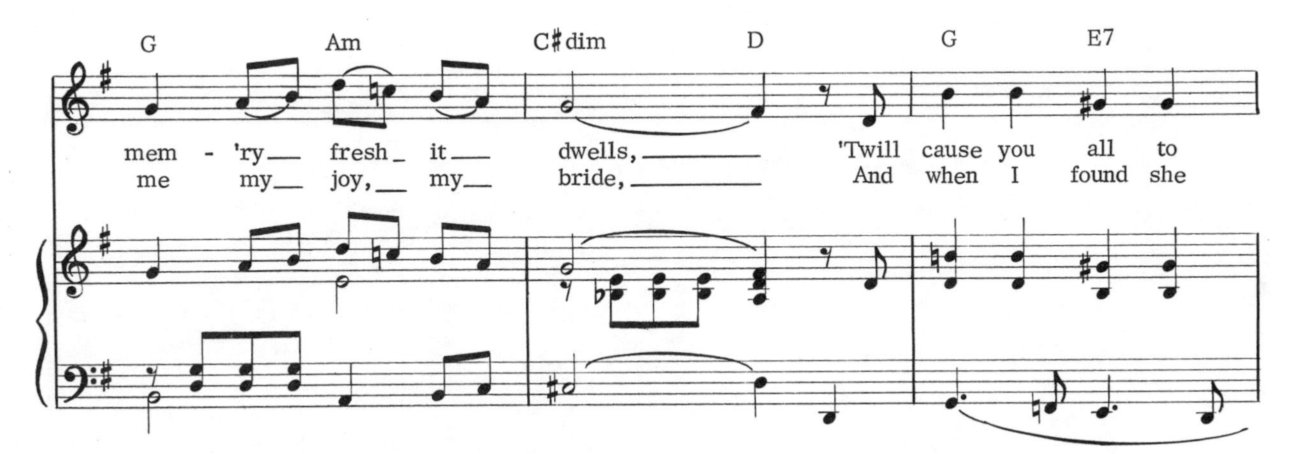
G Am C♯dim D G E7
mem - 'ry fresh it dwells, 'Twill cause you all to
me my joy, my bride, And when I found she

Am E7 Am G D7 G
drop a tear On the grave of my sweet Kit - ty Wells.
was no more, Then I laid my ban - jo down and cried.

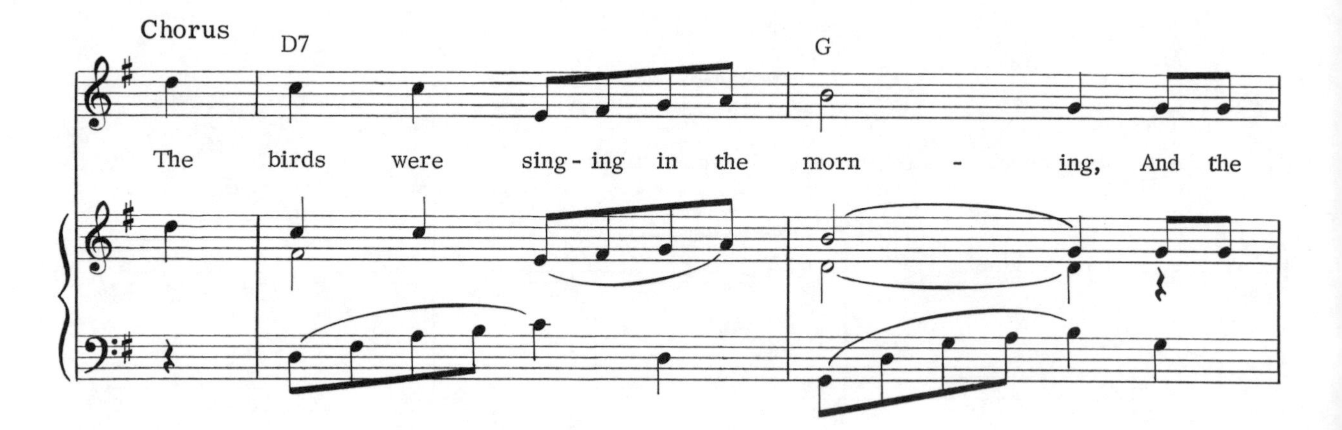

3. I often wish that I was dead
And laid beside her in the tomb;
The sorrow that bows down my head
Is silent in the midnight gloom.
The springtime has no charms for me
Though flowers are blooming in the dells,
For that bright form I do not see,
'Tis the form of my sweet Kitty Wells.

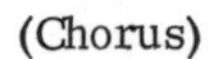
(Chorus)

Hymns and Sacred Songs

We're All Here: The Song of the Freed Men

Words and Music Traditional USA 1880

Pa's fingers were too stiff from being out in the cold for him to play the fiddle. In hard times before, he had made music for them; now there was none for him. Suddenly Laura remembered the chorus of "The Song of the Freed Men." "We're all here!" she exclaimed. "We can sing!" And she began to hum the tune. LW, *page 290*

3. As I go down the steps of time,
   Do thyselfa no harm,
   I leave this sinful world behind,
   Do thyselfa no harm.

   (Chorus)

4. If you get there before I do,
   Do thyselfa no harm,
   Tell them I am acoming too,
   Do thyselfa no harm.

   (Chorus)

Am I a Soldier of the Cross?

Words by Isaac Watts   Music by Reverend John Chetham   1724

Isaac Watts, an English Congregationalist pastor, wrote more than six hundred hymns. Many are still used today.

On Sundays Laura and Mary could not run or shout or be noisy in their play. They had to sit quietly and hold their dolls or look at pictures. At bedtime Pa would play and sing "Shall I be carried to the skies. . . ." LHBW, *page 97*

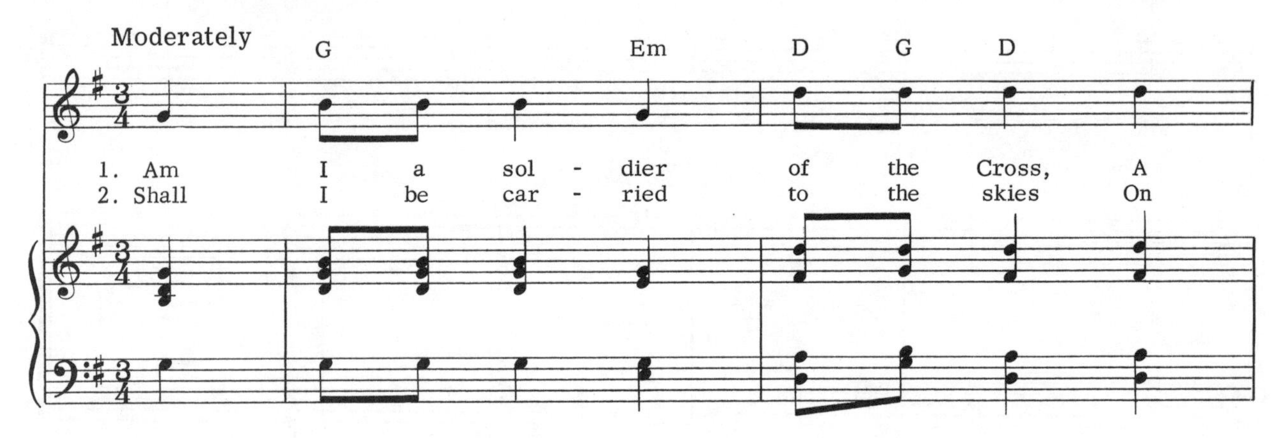

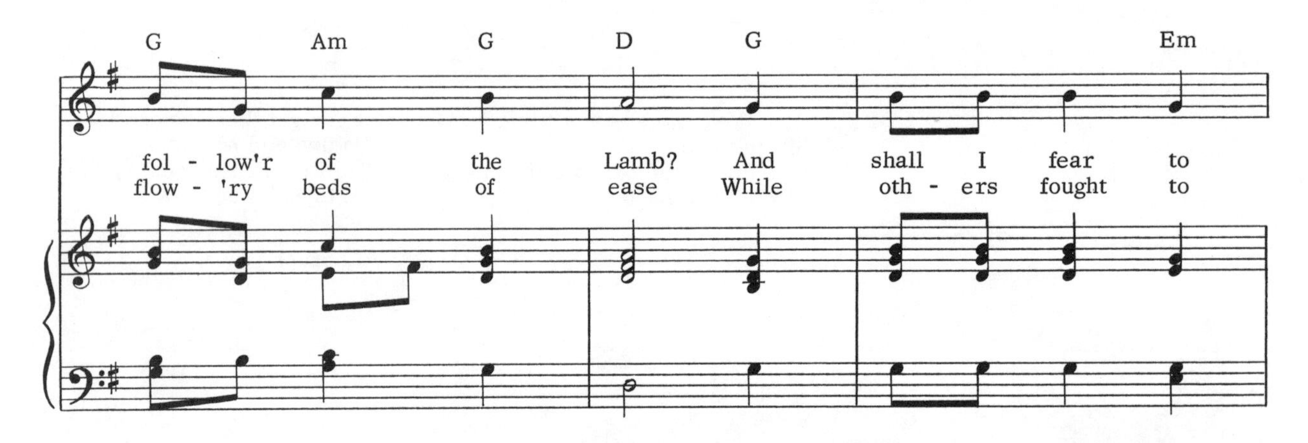

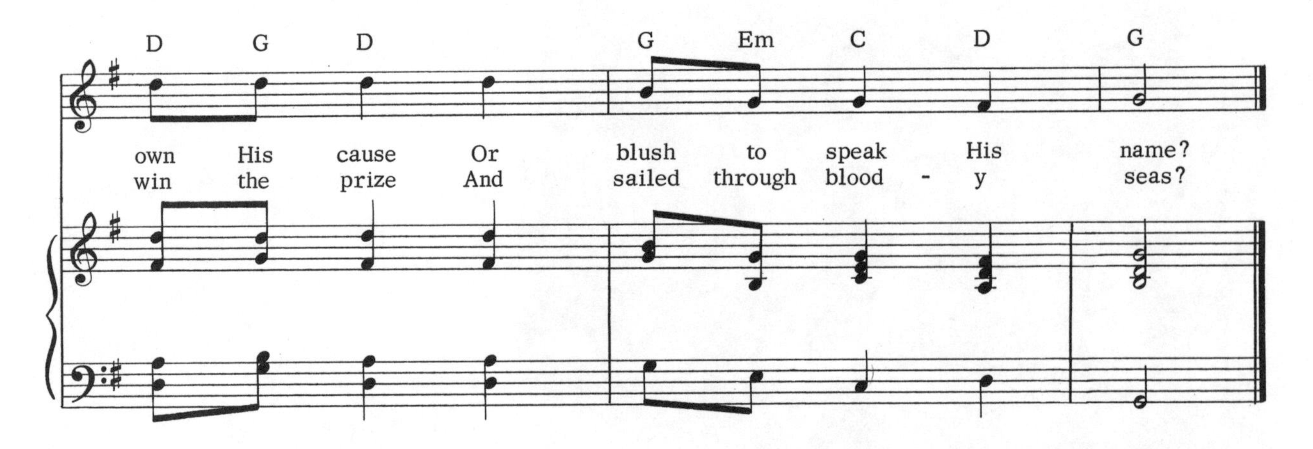

When I Can Read My Title Clear

Words by Isaac Watts   Music by J. P. Holbrook   *1709*

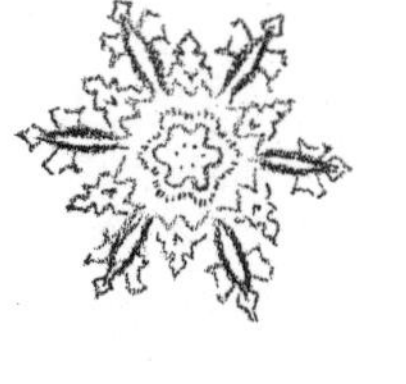

In addition to hymns and sermons, Isaac Watts was also the author of *Divine and Moral Songs for Children*, a celebrated book of juvenile verse.

On the first night of the four-day blizzard on the prairie, the storm raged outside, hammering at the walls and windows. But the family, safely sheltered and huddled in the warmth of a hay fire, went on singing. LW, *page 291*

Moderately

G D Em D G

1. When I can read my ti - tle clear
2. Should earth a - gainst my soul en - gage,

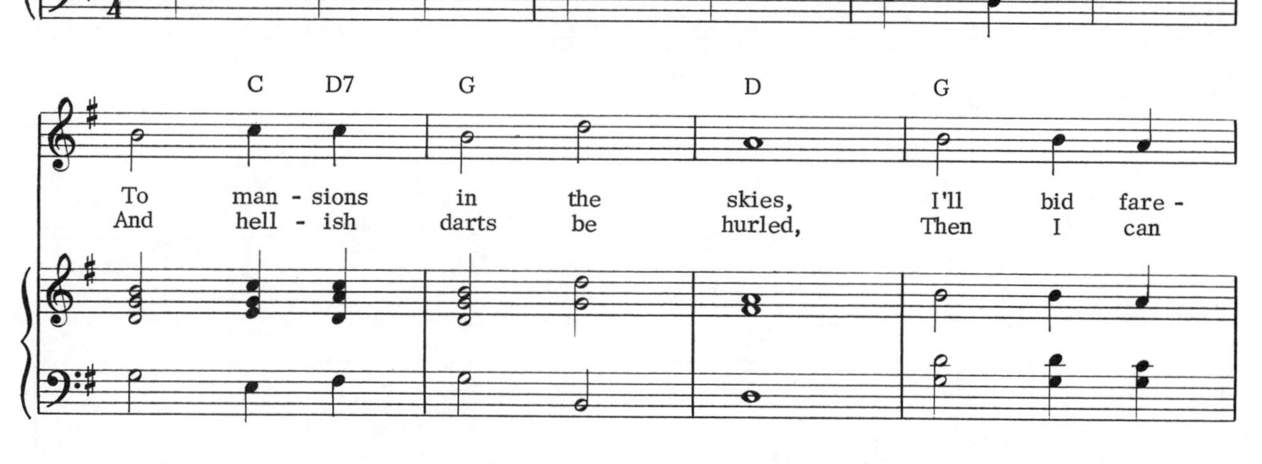

3. Let cares like a wild deluge come,
And storms of sorrow fall;
May I but safely reach my home,
My God, my heaven, my all.

4. There shall I bathe my weary soul
In seas of heavenly rest,
And not a wave of trouble roll
Across my peaceful breast.

The Home of the Soul

Words by Mrs. E. H. Gates   Music by Philip Phillips   1866

At the composer's request, the words to this song were written in the spirit of *The Pilgrim's Progress*, the famous allegory by John Bunyan.
The hymn blended with the wailing of the winds outside as Ma sat in her rocking chair and softly sang about the beautiful land "where no storms ever beat."
LW, *page 241*

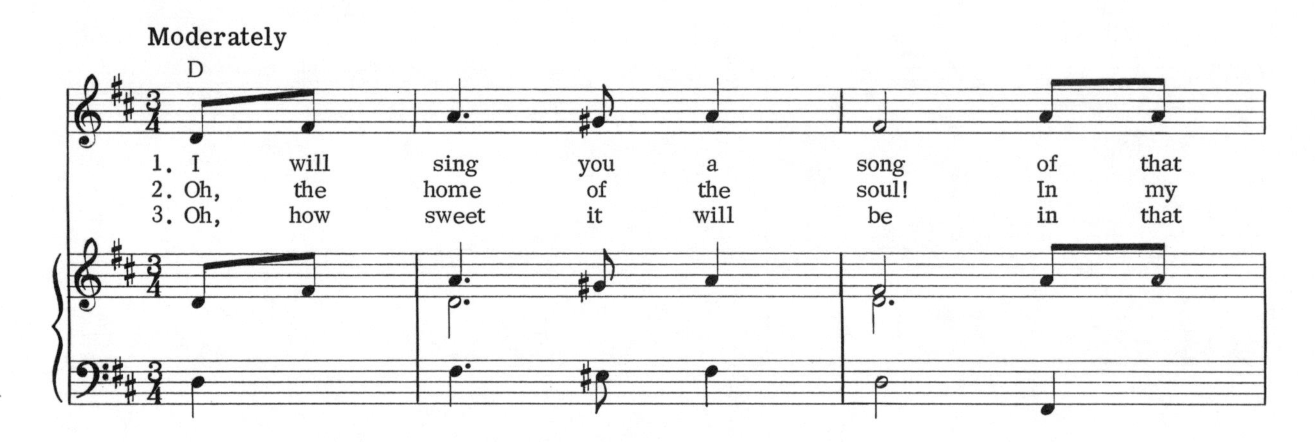

D
A7
D
strand While the years of e - ter - ni - ty roll.
venes Be - tween the fair cit - y and me.
hands, To meet one an - oth - er a - gain.
Chorus
A7
D
G
D
A
A7
While the years of e - ter - ni - ty roll, Where no
Be - tween the fair cit - y and me, Till I
To meet one an - oth - er a - gain, With
D
G
storms ev - er beat on the glit - ter - ing
fan - cy but dim - ly the veil in - ter -
songs on our lips and with harps in our
D
A7
D
strand While the years of e - ter - ni - ty roll.
venes Be - tween the fair cit - y and me.
hands To meet one an - oth - er a - gain.

Merry, Merry Christmas! *(A Christmas Carol)*

Words and Music by Mrs. T. J. Cook 1871

This carol has a hymnlike quality that makes it suitable for a church Christmas celebration like the wonderful one in Minnesota, where Laura saw her first Christmas tree and realized that everything on the tree was a present for some-one! BPC, *page 253;* SSL, *page 187*

(Em) D7 G D7 G
ev - 'ry - where! Cheer - i - ly it ring - eth through the air.
Verse
D G C D7
1. Why should we so joy - ful - ly Sing with grate - ful mirth?
2. Light for wea - ry wan - der-ers, Com - fort for th' op - pressed!
3. Deeds of Faith and Char - i - ty, These our off - 'rings be,
G C G D7 G
See, the Sun of Right - eous-ness Beams up - on the earth!
He will guide His trust - ing ones In - to per - fect rest.
Lead - ing ev - 'ry soul to sing Christ was born for me!

My Sabbath Home

Words by Dr. Christopher Ruby Blackall   Music by W. H. Doane   1871

The author, an army surgeon during the Civil War, wrote several Sunday-school songs in collaboration with W. H. Doane, who composed many hymns of the gospel type.

Laura sang this at home when she was a little girl and later in a real Sunday-school class. HGY, *page 41;* BPC, *page 298*

3. Here Jesus stands with loving voice,
Entreating me to come
And make of Him my earnest choice,
In this dear Sabbath Home.

(Chorus)

The Ninety and Nine

Words by Elizabeth D. Clephane   Music by Ira D. Sankey   1876

First published in an English magazine, this poem was little-known until Ira D. Sankey came upon it and set it to music. It became the most famous of his gospel songs.

In town everyone went to the revival meetings. There were hymns and prayers and preaching. Laura loved this hymn, but Reverend Brown's thunderous calls for repentance sent chills up her spine. LTP, *page 276*

3. But none of the ransomed ever knew
How deep were the waters crossed,
Nor how dark was the night that the Lord passed through
Ere He found His sheep that was lost.
Out in the desert He heard its cry,
Sick and helpless and ready to die,
Sick and helpless and ready to die.

4. "Lord, whence are those blood drops all the way
That mark out the mountain's track?"
"They were shed for one who had gone astray
Ere the Shepherd could bring him back."
"Lord, whence are Thy hands so rent and torn?"
"They are pierced tonight by many a thorn,
They are pierced tonight by many a thorn."

5. And all through the mountains, thunder-riven,
And up from the rocky steep
There rose a cry to the gate of Heaven,
"Rejoice! I have found My sheep!"
And the angels echoed around the throne,
"Rejoice, for the Lord brings back His own!
Rejoice, for the Lord brings back His own!"

The Old Chariot

Words and Music Traditional USA

A Salvation Army favorite of long ago, this song was based on a Negro spiritual. During the long winter, Pa and some of the men in town set out in a railroad handcar to clear the tracks for the snowbound train. Everyone joined in singing this as they pushed the handlebars up and down. LW, *page 107*

C
stop and take him in, If the sin - ner's in the way, we will
roll it o - ver him, If the Dev - il's in the way, we will
F
stop and take him in, If the sin - ner's in the way, we will
roll it o - ver him, If the Dev - il's in the way, we will
D. C. al Fine
C
C7
F
stop and take him in, And we won't drag on be - hind!
roll it o - ver him, And we won't drag on be - hind!

Sweet By and By

Words by S. Fillmore Bennett   Music by J. P. Webster   1867

This "Christian ballad," written for a collection of Sunday-school hymns, was adopted by Ira D. Sankey for use as a revival number.

After Sunday dinner, Pa played hymn tunes on his fiddle. They sang all afternoon while icy snow beat down upon the house. LW, *page 130*

3. To our bountiful Father above,
We will offer the tribute of praise
For the glorious gift of His love
And the blessings that hallow our days.

(Chorus)

Pull for the Shore

Words and Music by Philip Paul Bliss Circa 1873

The first words of this famous gospel song always made Laura want to laugh. She remembered how solemnly it had been sung by the tall thin man and the pudgy little one as they made their inebriated way from one to the other of De Smet's two saloons. LTP, *pages 52, 278*

G7
C
Drear was the voy - age, sail - or, now al - most o'er;
Heed not the storm - y winds, though loud - ly they roar;
Am
D7
G
Safe with - in the life - boat, sail - or, pull for the shore.
Watch the bright and morn - ing star, and pull for the shore.
Chorus
G
D
Pull for the shore, sail - or, pull for the shore!
D7
G
Heed not the roll - ing waves, but bend to the oar;

3. Bright gleams the morning, sailor; uplift the eye!
Clouds and darkness disappearing; glory is nigh!
Safe in the lifeboat, sailor, sing evermore,
Glory, glory, hallelujah! Pull for the shore!

(Chorus)

There Is a Happy Land

Words and Music by Reverend Andrew Young 1838

Andrew Young, a Scottish schoolmaster, wrote this beloved hymn for children. When Ma sang it, Laura didn't know she had fallen asleep. She thought shining angels had begun to sing with Ma and that she was listening to their heavenly voices. LHP, *page 220*

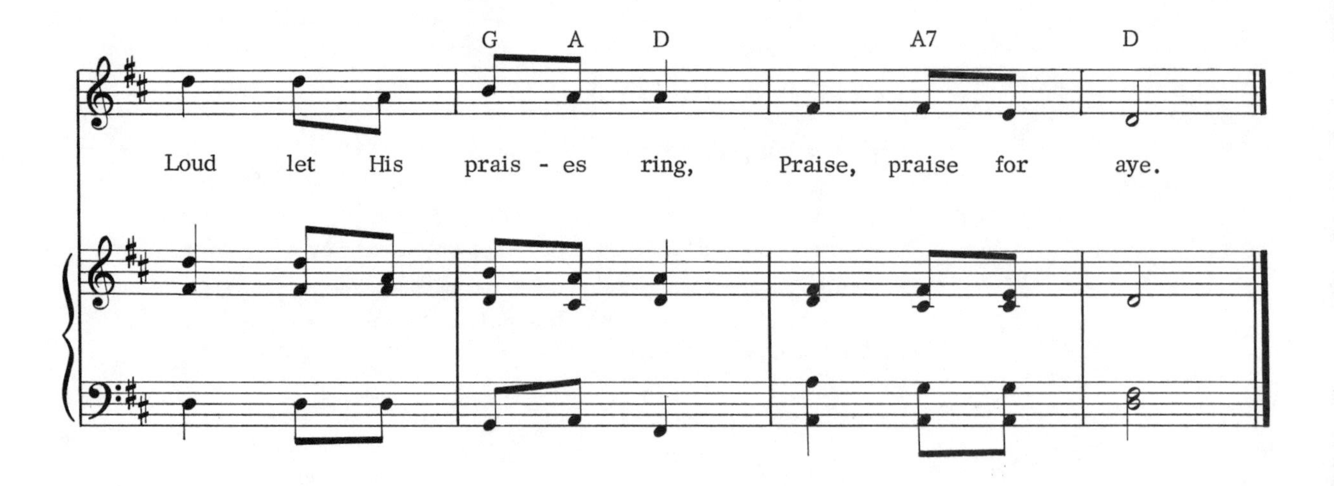

2. Come to that happy land,
   Come, come away;
   Why will ye doubting stand,
   Why still delay?
   Oh, we shall happy be
   When from sin and sorrow free,
   Lord, we shall live with Thee,
   Blest, blest for aye.

3. Bright, in that happy land,
   Beams every eye;
   Kept by a Father's hand,
   Love cannot die.
   Oh, then to glory run;
   Be a crown and kingdom won,
   And bright above the sun,
   We reign for aye.

Index

Song titles are listed in capital letters, first lines of songs in upper-and-lower-case roman.
First lines as they appear in the "Little House" books are in upper-and-lower-case italic.